# GALLIPOLI

KEVIN FEWSTER was born in Australia in 1953. He has been researching World War I for the past twenty years and from 1976 to 1979 he taught
history at the University of New South Wales, Royal Military College,
Duntroon. He holds a PhD from the University of New South Wales, was
the inaugural director of the Australian National Maritime Museum, and
is now the Director of the Powerhouse Museum in Sydney. Kevin Fewster
is the editor of *Gallipoli Correspondent: The frontline diary of C.E.W. Bean*,
published in 1983. He was made a Member of the Order of Australia in
2001 for services to museums and maritime heritage.

VECIHI BASARIN was born in İstanbul, Turkey in 1947. He trained in
Turkey as a chemical engineer and later lived and worked in Norway, the
United States, Brazil, Germany and the United Kingdom before migrating to Australia in 1973. He recently established his own consulting
company after working many years in energy and engineering related fields
as a manager.

HATICE HÜRMÜZ BASARIN was born in İzmir in Turkey in 1955.
She trained in Turkey as a town planner and migrated to Australia in 1979.
Since then she has completed a Masters degree in urban planning at the
University of Melbourne and has worked as a policy and research officer
on land use planning, local government and public housing related issues.

Vecihi Basarın and Hatice Hürmüz Basarın are coauthors of *The Turks
in Australia: Twenty-five years down under* which was published in 1993 to
celebrate the twenty-fifth anniversary of migration from Turkey. The
book focuses on the achievements of families on the very first migrant
charter flights that flew from Turkey to Australia in 1968. They have two
daughters, Zeynep and Alev.

# GALLIPOLI
## The Turkish Story

Kevin Fewster

Vecihi Başarın

Hatice Hürmüz Başarın

ALLEN&UNWIN

Allen & Unwin
83 Alexander Street
Crows Nest NSW 2065
Australia
Phone: (61 2) 8425 0100
Fax: (61 2) 9906 2218
Email: info@allenandunwin.com
Web: www.allenandunwin.com

National Library of Australia
Cataloguing-in-Publication entry:

Fewster, Kevin.
Gallipoli: the Turkish story.

Bibliography.
Includes index.
ISBN 1 74114 045 5.
ISBN 1 74114 161 3 (special edition)

1. World War, 1914–1918—Campaigns—Turkey—Gallipoli
Peninsula. 2. World War, 1914–1918—Turkey. I. Başarın,
Hatice Hürmüz, 1955– . II. Başarın, Vecihi, 1947– . III. Title.

940.426

Endpapers: This exceptionally fine, hand-knotted silk rug was produced in 1916, probably in
İstanbul, to commemorate the Ottoman victory at Çanakkale. Not only do the rug's colours coincide
with those frequently used on topographical relief maps, they also evoke very successfully the hues of
the coastline around the Gallipoli Peninsula. The rug is now owned by the esteemed Australian rug
dealer and collector, Mr Jacques Cadry. *Kindly lent by Jacques Cadry*

Set in 12/14 pt Granjon by Midland Typesetters, Maryborough, Victoria
Printed in Australia by McPherson's Printing Group

10 9 8 7 6 5 4 3 2 1

*For our parents and for John, who fought his own battle with courage and quiet dignity.*

# Contents

# List of maps

# Acknowledgements

Like our first book, this work is truly a cooperative effort. Not only did three of us combine to write it, we were greatly assisted by many others who generously offered their time, expertise and friendship. We are especially indebted to the Cadry family, Rabbi Jeffrey Kamins, Darel Hughes, Mr Peter King MP and Niyazi Adalı who first suggested we should revise and update our earlier work and who ensured we had the means to realise this ambition. John Iremonger, Ian Bowring, Emma Jurisich, Karen Penning and Catherine Taylor at Allen & Unwin enthusiastically supported us from the moment we first discussed the idea with them.

We also wish to thank our photo researcher, Carolyn Newman; Zafer Polat who provided source documents and photographs; Engin Aksaç who supplied material relating to Upfield Secondary College; Yüksel Yılmaz who helped publicise our Turkish community survey; John Mundy for advice about the Newfoundlanders at Gallipoli; Mahnur and Orhan Uğur for their assistance at Gallipoli; Kenan Çelik for advice on place names; Selçuk Kolay and Dr Mark Spencer regarding *AE2*; staff at Foto Balım in İzmir; staff at the Çanakkale Military Museum, and Major-General Steve Gower, Ashley Ekins and Peter Stanely at the Australian War Memorial.

We are grateful to Turkish Airlines and Ahmed Başar for their generous support of our project.

In addition, we wish to acknowledge those people who materially assisted us with the first version of this book: Ron Harper, Carmel Shute, Abdul Ayan, Necati Başarın, Barbara Helper, Marianne Graham, Harvey Broadbent, Ragıp Hanyal, Esen and Ertuğrul

Alparman, Dr Zofia Rueger and Kamuran Koyunoğlu. We were particularly indebted to Gallipoli veteran Mustafa Yıldırım and other members of Melbourne's Turkish community who graciously agreed to be interviewed for the book.

The following authors and publishers generously permitted us to quote from their books: CEW Bean, *The Official History of Australia During the War of 1914–18,* vols. 1 & 2, Angus and Robertson, Sydney, 1921, 1924; *Gallipoli Mission*, Australian War Memorial, Canberra, 1952; HM Denham, *Dardanelles: A Midshipman's Diary*, John Murray, London, 1981; R East, *The Gallipoli Diary of Sergeant Lawrence*, MUP, Carlton, 1981; Gammage, *The Broken Years*, ANU Press, Canberra, 1974; P Liddle, *Men of Gallipoli*, Penguin, London, 1976; A Moorehead, *Gallipoli*, illustrated edition, MacMillan, South Melbourne, 1975; J Murray, *Gallipoli 1915*, William Kimber & Co., London, 1965; M Tunçoku, *Anzakların Kaleminden Mehmetçik Çanakkale 1915*, Ankara, 1997; and cartoonist Bill Leak.

The source for each photograph used is acknowledged in its respective caption. We are especially grateful to the Australian War Memorial for permitting the use of so many images from its collections.

Finally, our greatest debt of thanks goes to Zeynep, Alev and Carol for their patience and unfailing support throughout the project.

# A note on terminology

Many 'Western' history books (including virtually all histories of the Gallipoli campaign) use the terms 'Ottomans' and 'Turks', and 'Ottoman Empire' and 'Turkey' as if they are interchangeable. The words may be synonymous to English-speaking peoples, but in fact they have quite specific historical meanings.

The Ottoman Empire was founded by a Turkish tribe in the fourteenth century AD. As it expanded, many other ethnic groups came under Ottoman control. By the time the empire reached its peak in the seventeenth century, the Turkish component of its population (most of whom lived in Anatolia) was probably a minority. Many other ethnic groups—Greeks, Kurds, Arabs, Bulgarians, Serbs, Croats, Albanians, Hungarians, Armenians, Macedonians and others—were also citizens of the empire.

In the early years of the empire, the Imperial Ottoman Court was mainly under the control of Turkish tribes but, as time passed, these other ethnic groups began asserting control over the affairs of state.

Many non-Muslims, who changed their name and their religion, served the sultan as administrators, trade or commercial agents, or in some other capacity. These people, called 'devshirme' (meaning converted or recruited), became an important political force. The sultan's harem followed the devshirme tradition. Many of its women were kidnapped, bought or offered as gifts from various parts of the empire. If not already Muslim, they were converted to Islam and given Muslim names. Some even mothered the imperial children. It is quite possible, therefore, that many of the sultans were of non-Turkish, non-Muslim blood.

The terms Turk and Turkish were adopted as nationalistic symbols by the Young Turks movement early in the twentieth century. This nomenclature became official orthodoxy in 1923 with the founding of the Republic of Turkey.

We decided to use the term Turk only where it applies specifically to Turkish people. Some of the Ottoman troops fighting on Gallipoli were not Turks, so we thought it best to refer to them as Ottomans. To have decided otherwise would have been like referring to Australians as 'the English'. In line with historical conventions, however, all quotations have been left in their original form. Thus, the words Turkish and English often appear when, in fact, the writers probably meant Ottoman and Australian.

For the sake of simplicity and consistency, the book uses the English names of places except where no suitable English equivalent exists or where the Allied commanders adopted the Turkish title.

# Place names on the peninsula

In the first column are the English names (if any) for prominent or significant features on and around the peninsula. Then come the Turkish names with pronunciation, and finally, an English translation of the Turkish names where appropriate.

| | | |
|---|---|---|
| Achi Baba | Alçı Tepe (Ul/che Te/peh) | |
| Anzac sector | Anafartalar (Anna/far/tala) | |
| Arı Burnu | Arı Burnu (Areh/ Boor/nooh) | |
| Baby 700 | Kılıç Bayır (Keh/lech Bah/yer) | Sword Ridge |
| Cape Helles | İlyasbaba Burnu (Ili/us bah/bah Boor/nooh) | |
| Chanak | Çanakkale (Chuh/nuk/kah/leh) | |
| Chunuk Bair | Conk Bayırı (Jonk Bah/yeh/reh) | |
| Constantinople | İstanbul (Is/tahn/bull) | |
| Dardanelles Straits | Çanakkale Boğazı (Chuh/nuk/ kah/leh Bo/ah/zeh) | The Straits of Çanakkale |
| Gaba Tepe | Kaba Tepe (Kah/bah Te/peh) | |
| Gallipoli | Gelibolu (Geh/lee/bo/looh) | |
| Hell Spit | Küçük Arı Burnu (Que/chuke Areh Boor/nooh) | Little Bee Point |
| Hill 971 | Koca Çimen Tepe (Ko/dja Chimen Te/peh) | Hill of the Great Pasture |
| Johnston's Jolly | Kırmızı Sırt (Ker/meh/ze Sehrt) | Red Ridge |
| Krithia | Kirte—now Alçıtepe (Ul/che Te/peh) | |
| Kum Kale | Kum Kale (Koom Kah/leh) | |
| Lone Pine | Kanlı Sırt (Kahn/leh Sehrt) | Bloody Ridge |

| | | |
|---|---|---|
| Maidos | Maydos—now Eceabat (Eh/je/ah/but) | |
| Mortar Ridge | Edirne Sırt (Ed/ear/neh Sehrt) | Adrianople Spur |
| The Pimple | Şehidler Tepesi (Sheh/hid/lehr Te/peh/sih) | Martyr's Hill |
| Plugge's Plateau | Hain Tepe (Hah/in Te/peh) | Cruel or Traitorous Hill |
| Quinn's Post | Bomba Sırt (Bom/bah Sehrt) | Bomb Spur |
| Russell's Top | Cesaret Tepe (Jez/sah/ret Te/peh) | Hill of Valour |
| The Nek | Boyun (Bo/yoon) | Neck |
| Salt Lake | Tuzla Gölü (Tooz/lah Gihr/lue) | Salty Lake |
| Sazli Dere | Sazlı Dere (Sahz/leh Deh/reh) | Reedy Creek |
| Sedd-el-Bahr | Seddülbahir (Said/dool/bah/here) | |
| Shrapnel Gully | Korku Deresi (Kohr/koo Deh/reh/sih) | Creek of Fear |
| Suvla Bay | Suvla Körfezi (Soov/lah Kerr/feh/zih) | |
| S Beach | Morto Koyu (More/toh Koh/yoo) | Morto Cove |
| V Beach | Ertuğrul Koyu (Ehr/too/rool Koh/yoo) | Ertuğrul Cove |
| W Beach | Teke Koyu (Te/keh Koh/yoo) | He-goat Cove |
| X Beach | İkiz Koyu (Ihk/kiz Koh/yoo) | Twin Cove |
| Y Beach | Pınarcık Koyu (Peh/nahr/jehk Koh/yoo) | Little Fountain Cove |

# Pronunciation of the Turkish alphabet

The modern Turkish alphabet has twenty-six letters and is written in Roman script. It does not have the letters *q, w* and *x* while it includes six letters which are not found in the English alphabet—*ç, ğ, ı, ö, ş, ü*. Each letter has only one sound. A pronunciation guide to the Turkish alphabet is provided below to assist the reader. Those letters which are pronounced the same way in English are not shown.

A a as *a* in far, car
C c as *j* in jaw, jelly
Ç ç as *ch* in chin, chew
E e as *e* in jetty, bed
G g as *g* in goat, get
Ğ ğ (silent g—never occurs at the beginning of a word) as *w* in rowing
I ı as *e* in answer, charter
İ i as *i* in sit, kit
J j as *zh* in treasure
O o as *o* in go, row
Ö ö as *i* in sir, fir
Ş ş as *sh* in shell, shout
U u as *oo* in book, look
Ü ü approximately as *u* in music

# Turkish/Ottoman history: A brief chronology

| | |
|---|---|
| Sixth century BC | Cyrus the Great, Emperor of Persia, invades central Asia where Turkic tribes live. |
| Fifth century AD | Huns of central Asia invade Europe through lands north of the Caspian Sea. (First major migration wave.) |
| Eighth century | Arabic/Islamic movements reach central Asia. |
| Eleventh century | Turkic tribes (including the Seljuks) begin moving westward from central Asia through lands south of the Caspian Sea. (Second major migration wave.) |
| 1071 | Battle of Malazgirt; Byzantine Empire unable to prevent Turkic tribes from entering Anatolia (modern-day Turkey) from the east. |
| Eleventh to thirteenth centuries | Seljuks (one of the Turkish tribes migrating westward) occupy most of eastern and central Anatolia. Crusaders try unsuccessfully to reverse this tide of occupation. |
| 1243 | Mongols invade and defeat Seljuks. Many small Turkic tribe/states are established in Anatolia, including the Ottoman tribe near Constantinople. Ottomans expand into north-west Anatolia. |
| 1357 | Ottomans capture the town of Gallipoli from the Byzantines and move to conquer the Balkans. |
| 1357–1451 | Ottomans expand influence in both Asia and Europe. |

| | |
|---|---|
| 1451–1566 | Ottomans conquer all of the Balkans, south of Russia, North Africa, Egypt and the whole of the Middle East and Arabian Peninsula. |
| 1453 | Ottomans capture Constantinople and rename it İstanbul. End of Byzantine Empire. |
| 1566–1683 | Period of stability. Ottoman borders extend from Vienna to Iran and from Crimea to Yemen. |
| 1683 | Ottomans lay siege to Vienna. Polish forces (and forces from other Germanic fiefdoms), called in by the Pope to assist the Austrian Empire to fight off the 'infidel Turks', defeat the Ottoman army. |
| 1683–1792 | Ottoman Empire in slow decline. |
| 1792–1878 | Rapid decline, Ottoman Empire becomes 'the sick man of Europe'. |
| 1853 | Crimean War. Ottomans join forces with Britain and France to repel Russian threat to İstanbul. |
| 1878–1908 | Brief period of stability. |
| 1908 | Young Turks revolution. |
| 1909–18 | Young Turks rule. |
| 1912–13 | Balkan Wars. Joint forces of Bulgaria, Greece and Serbia defeat Ottomans with relative ease. |
| 1914 | Turkey enters World War I. |
| 1915 | Gallipoli campaign. |
| 1918 | Defeated Ottoman Empire disintegrates. |
| 1919–23 | War of Liberation. |
| 1923 | Republic of Turkey declared. |
| 1968 | First government-assisted Turkish migrants arrive in Australia. |
| 2001 | 53 000 Australians describe themselves as being of Turkish ancestry (Census of Population and Housing, Australian Bureau of Statistics). |

# Introduction

The last surviving soldier of any of the armies that fought at Gallipoli in 1915 died peacefully in a Hobart nursing home on 16 May 2002, aged 103. Alec Campbell, a Tasmanian, lied about his age and enlisted, aged 16, to go off to war with the Australian Imperial Force (AIF). He landed at Gallipoli on 2 November 1915. Known affectionately as 'the Kid' to his soldier mates, he spent six weeks at the front before being evacuated. Soon after, he contracted enteric fever and was invalided back to Australia in 1916, too ill to fight. The last Turkish survivor died some years earlier while the final English veteran passed away a few months before Campbell.

Alec Campbell's death triggered a massive reaction across Australia. All major newspapers produced special supplements to commemorate the passing of this, the last Gallipoli Anzac. Australia's Prime Minister cut short his official visit to China to attend the state funeral in Hobart. At 11 a.m. on the day of his funeral, virtually the entire nation paused for a minute out of respect for Private Campbell and all those Australians who fought at Gallipoli and forged the Anzac legend.

Campbell was a reluctant hero. Only in his latter years did he attend Anzac Day commemorations and his family say he rarely spoke of the war. In the words of his wife, he symbolised 'the young soldiers of the time who went eagerly off to war only to return with very different emotions ... He saw the futility of war as would anyone who went to war'.[1] In rejecting official offers to erect a statue honouring his memory, the family emphasised that Alec Campbell not only shied away from glorifying war during his life, he also campaigned vigorously for peace.

Among the floral tributes laid outside Hobart's St David's cathedral was a wreath sent by a local Turkish association. Until recent years, it would have been seen as somewhat provocative for a local Turkish group to link itself to Australia's Anzac experience. But, over the past decade or so, there has been a remarkable change in the public mood of these one-time protagonists. Turks and Australians have seemingly buried their enmity and now see Gallipoli as a unique bond between the two nations. This mutual respect is aptly summed up by a small article that appeared in the *Sydney Morning Herald* the day after Campbell was buried. An Australian working in Montreal, Canada, had mentioned Campbell's death to a Turkish work colleague. The Turk replied about the Anzacs: 'In Turkey, we don't consider them as the enemy any more. They fought bravely, and Turkey is proud of the war fought on both sides. It was our greatest military victory. But your sons, buried in Turkey, are our sons.'[2]

It's quite likely that he made these remarks knowing that they paraphrased Mustafa Kemal Atatürk's immortal pronouncement almost seventy years ago:

> Those heroes that shed their blood and lost their lives. You are now living in the soil of a friendly country, therefore rest in peace. There is no difference between the Johnnies and the Mehmets to us where they lie side by side, here in this country of ours. You, the mothers, who sent their sons from faraway countries, wipe away your tears; your sons are now lying in our bosom and are in peace. After having lost their lives on this land, they have become our sons as well.[3]

Mustafa Kemal was the most imaginative, most successful officer to fight on either side at Gallipoli. At several moments in the campaign his personal intervention was almost certainly the difference between success and failure for the Ottomans. Gallipoli launched his career. He subsequently became the first president of the newly formed Republic of Turkey and the nation's acknowledged founding father.

In the past decade or so Australians have become increasingly willing to accept Turks and Turkey into the nation's annual remembrance of Anzac. This respect between Turk and Australian, born out of war against each other, is truly unique. Come Anzac Day each year, neither Australia's political leaders nor the RSL embraces the

Germans or Japanese as it does the local Turkish community. This book also attempts to explain why Australians and Turks now regard Gallipoli as the war that made them friends.

Virtually every Anzac Day sees the launch in Australia of at least one new book about Gallipoli. Invariably, they focus almost exclusively on the deeds of the Anzacs and, to a lesser degree, the other Allied armies which fought on that now famous peninsula. The armies that opposed them receive relatively scant attention; like support actors in a play, their appearance is essential for the show to go on, but rarely are they allowed to move on to centre stage. Turkish histories are much the same, with the balance reversed. Even if national chauvinism is disregarded, the lop-sided treatment in the Australian books is, in some ways, quite understandable. The Allies were the aggressors in the war—they were the invaders. Thus it is perhaps to be expected that 'Western' accounts concentrate primarily on the strategies and performance of those who initiated (and bungled!) much of the fighting.

But what of the victors? The Ottoman armies fought with great distinction on Gallipoli, yet, year after year, the overwhelming majority of children in Australia learn at school only the Anzac side of the Gallipoli story. This book attempts, in a small way, to redress this imbalance. It is as partisan as any other book on the subject, and for that we make no apologies. We deliberately set out to write a book that challenges the orthodox version of the campaign. We hope that our account of the events will encourage readers to reflect a little on the battles themselves, on the way the Anzac legend has evolved since, and on the role it and other legends serve in our society.

This book has grown out of an earlier book, *A Turkish view of Gallipoli—Çanakkale*, co-written by the same three authors in the early 1980s. Since then, major shifts have occurred both in how Australians feel about Anzac Day and how Australia's Turkish community responds to the Anzac legend and the annual rituals of Anzac Day. Faced with these changes, we thought it time to totally rework and update our earlier study.

All three authors came to this book with a strong personal anti-war commitment. In researching and writing the book, we have tried to strip away the glamour that is so often allowed to mask the terrible

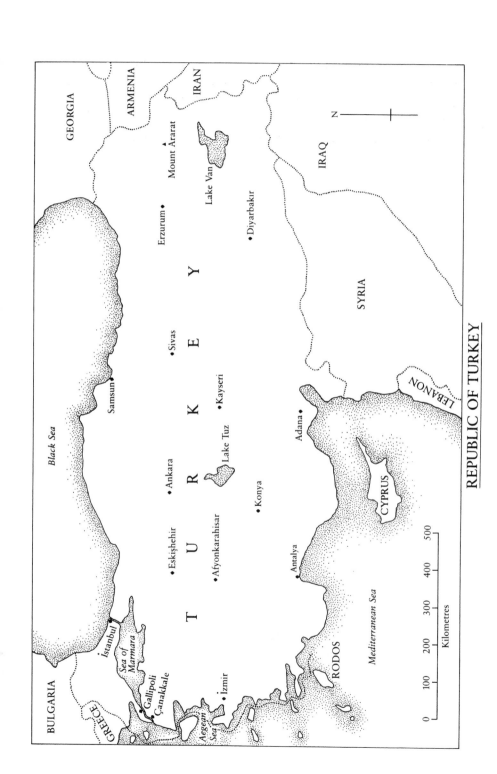

REPUBLIC OF TURKEY

reality of war. Through describing the somewhat similar ways in which Gallipoli has been nurtured as a potent nationalistic symbol in Australia, New Zealand and Turkey since 1915, we hope our readers might reassess the function that Gallipoli has served in helping shape the national culture and identity in each of these three countries.

# ONE

# A special bond

'Seldom have so many countries of the world, races and nations sent their representatives to so small a place with the praise-worthy intention of killing one another.'[1] This remark, made by a German officer who fought alongside the Ottomans at Gallipoli, aptly sums up the bloody reality of that famous campaign. Through-out 1915, Ottoman and German troops turned back repeated sea and land assaults from British, French, Indian, Newfoundland, Aus-tralian and New Zealand forces. In all, nearly a million men fought there. The battlefields were tiny; the casualties enormous. The Ottomans threw almost half a million men into the battle, of whom 250 000 became casualties. Although no accurate records are available, 86 000 Ottoman troops died there. The German contingent was very small and lost few men. British and Indian casualties totalled 119 696 (including over 28 000 dead); the French suffered 47 000 casualties. Australia's wounded numbered 27 700, of whom 8700 were killed, while the New Zealanders lost 7571 men (2701 killed). It seems almost incomprehensible that such casualties could be sustained in this small area. Almost 50 000 Australians subsequently died on the Western Front—when compared to that level of sustained butchery in battle, we are tempted to view the Gallipoli losses almost as light. The Ottomans, by comparison, suffered more casualties at Gallipoli than in any other campaign of the war. In many regards, all such comparisons are invidious. What comfort is it for a dead soldier's loved ones or the maimed to be told that Gallipoli was not quite the hell of France and Belgium? Not quite . . . but hell all the same.

In Turkey, the campaign is known as the Battle of Çanakkale.

This title connotes the phase of the campaign Turks reg[...]
significant. Çanakkale is the name of the town situated o[...]
side of the straits which Europeans call the Dardanelles. The Turks
view the campaign primarily as a battle for the Çanakkale straits
(known by Europeans as the Narrows), a battle which they won prin-
cipally because of the great naval victory they recorded in the straits
on 18 March 1915. Australians and New Zealanders, on the other
hand, remember the campaign as Gallipoli because their forces
fought a land campaign on the Gallipoli peninsula. Like the Turks,
they have chosen the name which emphasises their most significant
and most successful contribution to the battle. It is interesting to note
that the British and French, who fought in both the sea and land
battles, refer to the campaign as Gallipoli or the Dardanelles.

For the British, French, Canadians, Indians and Germans, the
Gallipoli campaign is remembered as just another name in a long,
tragic list of World War I battles. For Turks, Australians and New
Zealanders, Gallipoli is something apart—a significant event in the
self-development of their individual nations. Gallipoli occupies a
special place in the national memory. As such, the battles have not
been allowed to fade in people's memories. Each year, Australians
and New Zealanders remember their war dead on 25 April, the date
ANZAC (Australian and New Zealand Army Corps) troops first
landed on the Gallipoli peninsula. The occasion is set aside as a public
holiday, with veterans' marches and memorial services held in large
cities and small towns across the land. In Turkey, the annual commemoration centres around the decisive victory won over the British
and French fleet on 18 March 1915. It is not a public holiday but
senior government and military figures attend special ceremonies in
and around Çanakkale. In recent times, the Ottoman victory at
Gallipoli has been made the basis for Turkish nationalistic rhetoric,
and the religious aspect of the campaign (the fight against the infidel),
once utilised as the principal rationale for fighting the war, is no
longer even mentioned.

Nearly ninety years have passed since the campaign—thus four
generations have reflected on what happened and what it might
mean. Turkey now remembers the campaign, above all else, for
launching the career of Mustafa Kemal, the young officer who went

on to become Atatürk, the inaugural president and founder of modern Turkey. Kemal displayed brilliant leadership qualities at Gallipoli; his rapid appraisal of a situation and measured response proved, on several occasions, the difference between victory and defeat. Senior officers, jealous of his success, ensured that his deeds did not receive any public credit at the time. Kemal won almost all his victories against the Anzacs, yet his name was unknown to them until after the war. Today, the once unsung hero is acclaimed as the master general of the campaign. A massive concrete monument dominates Chunuk Bair commemorating his contribution to the Çanakkale victory. Busloads of Turkish tourists flock to the memorial. For them, and almost all Turks, Gallipoli is remembered first and foremost as a chapter in the life and legend of their nation's most famous son—Atatürk literally means 'father of the Turks'.

The passage of time has also affected how Australians perceive Gallipoli. People speak of it with such pride and feeling, you could

One of five huge concrete 'tablets' at Chunuk Bair that recount the deeds of Mustafa Kemal and his troops. The configuration of the monoliths symbolises a man's hand cupped towards the sky in prayer. *H. H. Başarın*

be mistaken for believing it was a great military victory, not a lamentable strategic blunder. Thus, when his yacht *Australia II* trailed three races to one in the 1983 America's Cup, Alan Bond (an English migrant) cheerfully told the press: 'We had our backs to the wall there [on Gallipoli], and we won that one.' Another Australian had to remind him that Gallipoli was a military tragedy salvaged only by a mass withdrawal. The defiant Bond then added that what he meant by the Anzac analogy was that Australians do not give up without a fight.[2] It was an easy error to make; the campaign is generally described in terms which highlight the strengths of the Anzacs' performance and skate over their shortcomings. The Anzacs are praised for the landing and evacuation, acclaimed for capturing the redoubtable Ottoman trenches at Lone Pine, and pitied for being led by British officers, many of whom are claimed to have been half-witted. Australia's Gallipoli, as portrayed in Australian director Peter Weir's highly successful feature film of the same name, is remembered as a triumph of the Australian character over a hostile foe, difficult terrain and incompetent leadership. The Turks might have won the battle but we won the fight, is what most Australians like to believe. There are grains of truth in all these observations, but they also contain many fallacies and a good deal of folklore.

After Gallipoli, generations of Australians perceived the Turks as dour, determined people. In 1983, for example, a Melbourne journalist wrote: 'The Turks, of course, are incredibly dogged, a fact known to every grandparent and schoolchild since 1915. They dug their toes in at Gallipoli and they've dug them in now at the City Square.'[3] The newspaper was reporting on a hunger strike staged in central Melbourne by nine Turkish men attempting to persuade the Australian Government to sever diplomatic relations with Turkey's then repressive military government.

Over the two decades since then, a sea change has occurred in Australian–Turkish relations. Gallipoli is for most Australians still their primary point of contact with Turkey and Turkish people. But now the 1915 battles are seen as things that bond the two nations. A new respect, even a sentimentality, has emerged with 'Johnny Turk' today being a figure much more loved than hated by Australians. In Australia and Turkey, it has almost become obligatory to mention

Gallipoli whenever the other country is the subject matter. For example, Victorian Premier Steve Bracks, when dispatching a mobile medical caravan in July 2001 to the victims of the 1999 earthquake in Turkey, said: 'Australians share a special bond with Turkey that goes back to another terrible experience at Gallipoli. And that shared experience makes our community effort even more meaningful.'[4]

Despite the passing of the years, the Gallipoli story is still passed down with the same passion as in earlier generations. Australian schoolchildren still listen to stories of brave Simpson and his donkey, the gallant attack at Lone Pine, the selfless charge at the Nek, or some such tale of Australian bravery. Each year the children are asked to observe a minute's silence in memory of men and events they probably do not understand. No-one could pass through the Australian education system without becoming aware of Gallipoli, but few students realise that the Anzacs were invaders. Even after all

This German-made gun, reputedly used at Gallipoli, was brought to Australia after World War I and placed in a park in Maldon, Victoria. It was restored by the local RSL sub-branch as its 1988 bicentenary project. *V. Başarın*

A similar gun in action on Gallipoli in 1915. *AWM A05287*

these years, the Anzac legend, like all legends, is highly selective in what it presents as history.

The interesting thing is that, in some ways, the legend has been redefined in recent years to embrace the Turkish soldiers along with the Anzacs. In recent times, Australia's annual Anzac Day remembrance has focused less on the battles and more on the human values that shone through during the fighting. When viewed in this light, the Anzac and Ottoman soldier can each be seen as sharing much the same fate; fellow sufferers rather than sworn enemies. This sense of a shared experience between the soldiers of the two countries has created a special affinity between the two nations. The retiring NSW RSL President, Rusty Priest, highlighted this point in 2002 when he addressed a special event staged in his honour by the Consul-General of Turkey and the NSW Council of Turkish Associations. In Mr Priest's words, 'Australia and Turkey are perhaps the only two countries in the world that have a strong friendship born out of a war.'[5]

In saying this, he was echoing similar sentiments expressed by Turkey's Prime Minister, Bülent Ecevit, at the eighty-fifth anniversary commemorations held at Anzac Cove in April 2000.[6]

The 1915 Gallipoli battles have undoubtedly been the major factor in fostering closer ties of friendship between Australians, New Zealanders and Turks at both national and local levels over the past decade or so. The first steps along this path were taken in 1985 when a small group of Australian veterans returned to Gallipoli as guests of both governments to commemorate the seventieth anniversary of the campaign. The Turkish government announced it was officially renaming Arı Burnu beach Anzac Cove. Australia reciprocated by naming a park near the Australian War Memorial in Canberra as well as a stretch of coastline near Albany in Western Australia (where the first Australian Imperial Forces convoy sailed in 1914) after Kemal Atatürk. For its part, New Zealand renamed a prominent piece of land near the entrance to Wellington Harbour in honour of Atatürk.[7]

Arı Burnu beach, officially renamed Anzac Cove by the Turkish government in 1985. *H. H. Başarın*

Australian veteran, Jack Ryan, embraces a Turkish veteran at the
75th anniversary commemoration at Gaba Tepe, 1990. *Commonwealth Department of Veterans Affairs*

The seventy-fifth anniversary of the campaign attracted even
greater attention. Fifty-four Australian and six New Zealand
veterans, accompanied by the Australian Prime Minister, Bob
Hawke, and the New Zealand Governor-General were joined by
political leaders from Turkey and Britain plus around 10 000 people
who gathered for the dawn service at Anzac Cove. Hawke was the
first incumbent Australian prime minister ever to visit Turkey. The
anniversary attracted enormous publicity, in particular, the Australian Broadcasting Corporation's televising of the dawn service live

back to Australia. The seven-hour time difference meant that the live coverage of the Anzac Cove ceremony commenced on Australia's eastern seaboard at lunchtime, just after the major Anzac Day marches had finished.

During the day's program, at Lone Pine, Prime Minister Hawke unveiled a bronze information plaque researched and produced by Dr Ross Bastiaan, a Melbourne dentist and Army Reserve officer with a deep personal commitment to honouring Australia's war dead. Bastiaan had conceived the idea after visiting Gallipoli in 1987 and being disappointed by the lack of information for English-speaking visitors. He spent the next three years negotiating with the Turkish government to gain their approval. With support from numerous major Australian corporations, he produced ten plaques, each in four languages—English, Turkish, German and French— that were mounted at important locations between Anzac Cove and Hill 971. Bastiaan has subsequently produced similar plaques for every battlefield across the world in which Australians have fought.

Among the thousands in the crowd at Anzac Cove that day was a Turkish academic, Professor Mete Tunçoku. A few weeks earlier he had organised an international conference in Ankara discussing aspects of the Gallipoli campaign. Standing in the cold half-light of the early morning, he recalls:

> I was deeply touched when I observed the excitement and tearful eyes of those old soldiers landing in boats on the coast of Gallipoli before dawn just as it had been 75 years ago. But, this time they were greeted by their Turkish friends with embraces and gifts and flowers. It was an unforgettable scene for all of us . . .
>
> [A] pall of melancholy and sorrow hung over everything. Interestingly enough, there was no enmity or anger . . . You could have thought they were old friends who had just met after a very long time . . .
>
> On that day, I met a very old Turkish veteran and an Anzac veteran standing side by side. The Turkish veteran was trying to stand up straight with the help of his walking stick. The old Anzac was looking around with tears in his eyes. Surely, both of them were thinking of the terrible days of the war and of the friends they had lost. At one moment, I saw the Turkish veteran gently putting his conspicuously veined big boned hand on the shoulder of the Anzac who, weeping silently, watched the hills and slopes. I remained speechless and rooted to the spot . . . This scene was the obvious

expression of the meaning of Çanakkale battles. Evidently, the veteran was
trying to tell his friend through that touch, what he was unable to put into
words . . .[8]

Tunçoku was so moved by the event he decided to make a study of
the Turkish and Anzac veterans and their seemingly deep mutual
respect. He visited Australia and New Zealand in 1991 and questioned twenty-seven elderly Anzacs on what they knew about
Turkey before the war, how much contact they had with the Turks
during the battles, and if their views had changed since the war.
Nearly all of them described their Ottoman opponents as brave and
fair, or words similar. Sixteen of his respondents had made the 1990
pilgrimage back to Gallipoli. One of them, JJ Ryan of Sydney,
recounted his own special moment at the seventy-fifth anniversary
commemorations. During one of the battles, Ryan had captured
three Ottoman soldiers—'easy going fellows, not too happy to be
captured'. He removed their trouser belts 'to stop any chance of
escape'.[9] He'd kept the belt buckles as souvenirs and took them back
to Turkey with him in 1990, presenting them to a Turkish official
who reciprocated by presenting him with a special plaque. 'I subsequently served in France,' 96-year-old Ryan told Tunçoku, 'but still
remember more of [the] Turkish campaign than other battles.'[10]

Virtually every year since 1990, either the Governor-General,
Prime Minister or a senior government minister has represented the
Australian people at the Anzac Cove service. The eighty-fifth
anniversary in 2000, for example, saw both the Australian Prime
Minister and Turkish President in attendance. And it is not just in
Australia and Turkey that this new spirit of camaraderie is evident.
Australian and New Zealand diplomatic missions across the world
all commemorate Anzac Day in some way or other. In 1999, Ms
Buket Uzuner, author of the first Turkish novel about Gallipoli,
*Gelibolu ve Uzun Beyaz Bulet* (Gallipoli and the Long White Cloud),
a story about a New Zealander's journey to Gallipoli in search of her
great-grandfather killed in the battles, was invited in what she
termed 'an honourable gesture' to attend the ceremony at the New
Zealand Consulate in New York.[11] In many places, the Australasian
missions stage a joint remembrance service. Such was the case in

Beijing, China, in 2002, where the two ambassadors, their staff, visitors and members of the local Australian and New Zealand expatriate communities came together in the courtyard of the Australian Embassy to mark Anzac Day. The ambassadors also invited their Turkish equivalent to solemnly read aloud Atatürk's immortal lines comforting the mothers of those from all nations who lost their lives and now lie in peace beneath Turkey's soil.

Within Turkey, recognition of the Anzacs has increased markedly in recent years, probably because of the annual influx of antipodean visitors, official and unofficial. Where Turkish school texts once described the enemy as consisting solely of English and French forces, school history books now make a point of identifying Australia and New Zealand's Anzac contingents. In the late 1990s, Australian historian Alan Moorehead's now classic account of the campaign, *Gallipoli*, was translated into Turkish and marketed for 'people who wish to learn more about the other side of the trenches'.[12] In 2001, the Ankara State Opera and Ballet company staged *Gallipoli*

Cartoonist Bill Leak's comment on Australian politicians' much publicised trips to Anzac Cove. *The Australian*, 29 April 2000.

*Martyrs*, especially choreographed as a call for world peace and to commemorate the Turkish, British, French, Anzac and Indian troops who fought there.[13] But perhaps the ultimate symbol of recognition came in 2002 as a leading Turkish daily newspaper, *Cumhuriyet*, sought to describe the powerfully unifying effect that Turkey's strong performance in soccer's World Cup was having across the nation. The paper sensed that the usual club versus club and player versus player rivalries had been put aside. People across Turkey were using the word 'us' when describing the national team's victories 'because the 23 [Turkish players] . . . in Korea were wearing the same colours, red and white, as the flag of Mustafa Kemal and his friends when they stopped the British, French and the Anzacs at Çanakkale'.[14]

In Australia, four years after the first plane-load of government assisted migrants arrived from Turkey, a small group of nine Turks marched in Sydney's 1972 Anzac Day parade behind the banner: 'Turkish Australian friendship will never die'. The idea to march come from Kemal Döver, who had arrived in Sydney with his wife and three sons as assisted migrants on the very first flight from Ankara in October 1968. Before coming to Australia, Döver had been a truck driver and a former Turkish heavyweight wrestling champion. In Australia, Kemal and his wife, Melahat, worked in factories. Sadly, Kemal was killed in a car accident in the late 1980s. Some years later, Melahat was interviewed about her family's life in Australia. Regarding his Anzac Day initiative, she recalled:

When we first came my husband got involved in community affairs. Associations were set up. He was a good orator. On our first or second Anzac Day here, he marched with a Turkish flag. Others said he was mad to do so. Telling them that Turks hadn't invited the Anzacs to Gallipoli, he marched and everybody clapped. He was the first one to do that. Then after a few years he gave up. Nobody marches now [then?]. Instead of uniting and telling the government their problems, members of the Turkish community were pulling in different directions. My husband felt frustrated that his efforts weren't appreciated.[15]

In the early 1980s, a decade after the groundwork had been laid in 1972, local Turkish groups again began seeking ways to involve

themselves in their adopted country's Anzac Day rituals. Undoubtedly, their motives were many and varied: to celebrate their own
heritage as it relates to Gallipoli, to acknowledge the sacrifices made
by the Anzacs, and to find common ground which might foster their
own integration into Australia's multicultural society.

At first these overtures were largely rejected. Melbourne is home
to Australia's largest Turkish community and when the idea was first
mooted in the early 1980s that Turks might participate in Melbourne's Anzac Day march, the State's RSL President, Bruce Ruxton,
stated bluntly: 'Anyone that was shooting us doesn't get in.'[16] Unde-
terred, various Melbourne Turkish groups started up their own
Anzac Day memorial function. Anzac Day marches across Australia
are organised by the local RSL branches, thus any change to the day's
format requires their consent. Rather than allow the Turks to march,
the RSL invited young Turks to join a young people's guard of
honour to line the World War I march to Melbourne's Shrine of
Remembrance. Over sixty young Turkish–Australians, dressed in
Turkish national costumes, joined groups of schoolchildren, school
cadets, scouts, Legacy children and others along the route.

A small contingent of Turkish migrants march in Sydney's Anzac Day parade,
1972.

In the mid-1990s, the Victorian RSL branch finally recognised changing community opinion and invited two representatives of the local Turkish returned soldiers association to join the Melbourne march. New South Wales soon followed Victoria's lead. In both cases, the Turks were permitted to march because they were Australia's ally in Korea, not because of their Gallipoli link, but one suspects this distinction was made for purely 'technical' reasons. The same year that Turks first marched in Melbourne's Anzac Day procession, Bruce Ruxton visited Turkey as the official guest of the Turkish veterans' association. Soon thereafter, Ruxton's committee decided that because Turks and Australian diggers had served alongside each other in the Korean War, a Turkish sub-branch of the RSL could be established in Melbourne. Turks now march in Melbourne, Canberra and Sydney's Anzac Day parade every year. To mark the eighty-fifth anniversary in 2000, the Turkish Ambassador arranged for a unique Ottoman Marching Band to participate in the Canberra march. This initiative was not without its problems, however, as the Ottomans traditionally march to a slower beat than the Australians and, apparently, this caused minor mayhem to the order of the procession! In 2002, a small Turkish group joined the Hobart march for the first time. It seems only a matter of time before Turks march in every major Anzac Day procession across Australia.

Now that the last Gallipoli Anzac has passed away, their medals are proudly worn in the Anzac Day march each year by their children, or their grandchildren, or their great-grandchildren. While these marchers do not have any direct experience of Gallipoli, they march out of respect for the men who earned the medals and the values they fought for. Rusty Priest defines the Anzac values as 'compassion, understanding and thinking of others',[17] while for the journalist and Gallipoli author, Les Carlyon, the Anzac tradition means 'refusing to give up no matter how hopeless the cause, it means looking after your mates, keeping your sense of humour, improvising and making do'.[18] With the passing of all the veterans, it seems probable that Anzac Day will continue to hold its special place in Australian hearts only if it becomes a celebration of these values rather than a day to cheer the mighty warrior. As such, Australia's Turks should be as welcome as anyone else to participate. Thirty-five years after Turkish migrants first came to Australia in large numbers, Australia's Turkish communities undoubtedly now feel that Gallipoli gives them a special tie with their new homeland. In addition to marching on Anzac Day, it is becoming commonplace for Turkish–Australian youth groups to travel to Atatürk Park in Canberra or even visit Gallipoli itself. Invariably, the students must submit lengthy assignments on their return home analysing their impressions. The dual loyalties felt by these young people are well summed up by the comments of students from Melbourne's Upfield Secondary College who reflected after visiting the battlefields:

> When I was at Gallipoli, I prayed for soldiers of both sides. It was unbelievable how the Australian soldiers, to prove themselves, attacked the hill knowing they would be dead.
>
> Anzacs lost the war but it was good to know that like the Turkish soldiers they also fought heroically to represent their country.[19]

Along with Auburn in Sydney, the Coburg-Moreland area of Melbourne is the nation's most readily identified centre of Turkish culture, thus it was perhaps not surprising that the Moreland Turkish Education and Social Affairs Centre's large float in Melbourne's 2001 Centenary of Federation parade, called Roots of Friendship, featured a Turkish and an Australian soldier exchanging water and cigarettes during a momentary ceasefire on Gallipoli. Another reflection of this emerging bond is that when the long-serving RSL state presidents in NSW and Victoria, Rusty Priest and Bruce Ruxton, retired in early 2002, special functions were organised by the Turkish Consuls General in Sydney and Melbourne honouring each man's 'invaluable contribution to the historic and everlasting relationship between Australian and Turkish traditional establishments'.[20]

In his acceptance speech at the Sydney reception, Rusty Priest told a story that captures perfectly the twin loyalties felt by many young Turkish–Australians. During Priest's term as RSL State President, he persuaded the State government to rename Sydney's imposing new Glebe Island Bridge the Anzac Bridge. From Armistice Day 1998, the bridge's two massive 'A-shaped' towers have flown an Australian and a New Zealand flag. Its Anzac symbolism was taken one step further when the NSW Roads and Traffic Authority was persuaded to commission a 4.2-metre bronze statue of a World War I digger. Priest conspired with the sculptor, Alan Somerville, to leave a small cavity beneath the figure's left boot. The statue was duly produced and its ceremonial unveiling organised for Anzac Day 2000 at the Bridge's western approach. Quite coincidentally, the crane operator who was contracted to lift the large sculpture into position was the Australian-born son of Turkish parents. Just before the lift was about to commence, Priest stepped forward and announced he had a small canister of sand he had collected some years earlier at Anzac Cove which he proposed to place under the soldier's foot. According to Priest, the young crane driver, overcome by emotion, had tears in his eyes as he skilfully manoeuvred the figure into place.

Many Australians now seek to experience first-hand the special link that Gallipoli gives to the Australia–Turkey friendship. Until the late 1980s, no more than a steady trickle of Australians ventured to Gallipoli. In fact, Betty Roland, a Victorian, mentions in her book *Lesbos, the Pagan Island* that she was the only person at Lone Pine and Gallipoli on Anzac Day 1961.[21] Following the much-publicised seventy-fifth anniversary commemorations in 1990, this trickle has turned into a flood. Around 60 000 Australians now visit Turkey each year; between 15 000 and 20 000 of them descend on Anzac Cove for the dawn service on 25 April. Why has there been such a dramatic upsurge in interest? First and perhaps foremost, many more Australians, especially young adults, are travelling overseas. Turkey is an attractive destination, offering fascinating cultural, historical and geographical attractions at a much lower price than most parts of Europe. While acknowledging these practical realities, it also has to be said that there has undoubtedly been an upsurge in interest, especially among young Australians, in the Gallipoli story, which has led to the peninsula becoming a site of pilgrimage for many Australians.

Two Australian academics, Dr Bruce Scates and Dr Raelene Frances, have studied the backpacker Anzac phenomenon and concluded that most young pilgrims are drawn to Gallipoli partly by the mystique engendered through films such as *Gallipoli* but also often through identifying with original Anzacs of their own age, their own name, or who came from their town or a town like it. Many young people, the study suggests, retrace the steps of their ancestors to

Something for everyone! As well as pointing you in the right direction, these roadside vendors will gladly sell you olives and tomatoes. *H. H. Başarın*

reclaim a part of their own heritage.[22] Turkey's media is certainly baffled by the motives of the youthful Anzac pilgrims. In recent years, Turkish papers have carried several stories in late April admitting an inability to understand why young backpackers spend thousands of dollars to be present at the dawn service, yet once there they get very drunk and unruly on the eve of such a sombre ceremony.

Any visitor to the Gallipoli peninsula today cannot help but be aware of the 1915 battles. While some battlefield tours leave from İstanbul most groups first assemble in Çanakkale, on the Asian side of the Narrows. In 1915, Çanakkale was a town of 16 000 people; today it's home to nearly 76 000. Local businesses welcome the visiting Australians and New Zealanders: you might choose to stay at the Hotel Anzac, dine at the Kiwi Restaurant or Anzac Büfe and book your tour through the Troy-Anzac Travel Agency. One local pension (small hotel) tries to set the scene by offering a special package which includes a screening of the Mel Gibson film *Gallipoli* the night before your tour!

Massive memorials to the fallen dot the landscape. The headland

Springtime in the Anzac Cemetery, Shrapnel Valley. *K. Fewster*

at Cape Helles, for example, is dominated by the 41 metre tall Çanakkale Martyrs Memorial honouring the 250 000 Ottoman soldiers who died in the 1915 battles. Travellers taking the ferry across the Narrows between Çanakkale and Eceabat (Maidos) see great Turkish memorials on each shoreline: on the Asian side a large sign simply cites the critical date 18 March 1915, while on the European hills thousands of white rocks have been arranged in the shape of a soldier with an accompanying message: 'Traveller, pause a moment to remember the dead'. Coming ashore from the ferry at Eceabat, you see the signs, in English, erected in the town square by the Commonwealth War Graves Commission directing non-Turkish-speaking visitors to the various Allied cemeteries.

In all, there are thirty-two Allied cemeteries on the peninsula, twenty-one of them clustered around Anzac Cove. The two main Anzac memorials are located on the site of each nation's most famous engagement: at Lone Pine for Australia, and on the crest of Chunuk Bair for the New Zealanders. Their walls list the names of those many

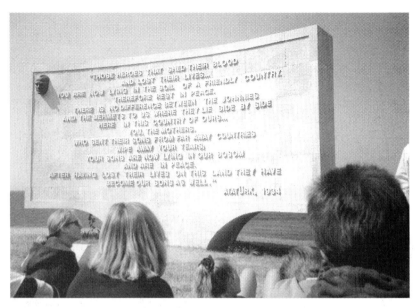

'Your sons are now lying in our bosom and are at peace . . .' Mustafa Kemal's famous message, sent in 1934 to the first group of official visitors from Australia, New Zealand and Britain, are immortalised on one of the huge monuments built by the Turkish government in the mid-1980s overlooking the sea near Anzac Cove. *V. Başarın*

thousands of soldiers who lie in unknown graves. Individual head-stones of Australian and New Zealand men are found in practically every cemetery. The green lawn plots studded with small memorial plaques and flowers are kept in immaculate condition by a team of Turkish gardeners working for the Commonwealth War Graves Commission. The Turkish cemeteries are less formal, but can usually be recognised from a distance by the rows of cypress trees always found at Turkish cemeteries. These cemeteries have never been main-tained to the same standard as the Allied war graves. None of the Turkish dead have individually marked headstones. One Turkish visitor to the area in 1925 commented:

> The sea was cheerful as if she did not remember anything; the earth was
> covered by deep green scrub from one end to the other as if it did not embrace

The reminders of battle are gradually fading. When this photo was taken in 1982, the remains of this landing craft were still clearly identifiable at North Beach. Twenty years later only a few ribs remain. *K. Fewster*

the young bodies of thousands of men . . . Only the foreign cemeteries were like white flower gardens on the sides of hills close to the sea. The only visible traces are not of those who won but those who were defeated.[23]

Perhaps responding to such comments, in recent years the Turkish government has erected a number of imposing new monuments honouring their fallen soldiers. The most impressive is at Chunuk Bair where five large white columns symbolise a man's hand turned upwards as if in prayer.

Curious tourists in search of less formal reminders of the battles can still see much of interest. The metal ribs of one landing craft still stand at the water's edge just north of Arı Burnu where the boat grounded in the shallows that fateful April morning long ago. A local man has, for many years, been collecting campaign relics and displaying them at a small museum in the village of Alçıtepe. The entire battle zone around Arı Burnu and parts of Suvla and

Three young backpackers (an Australian, a New Zealander and a Turk) pose for the camera in the re-constructed trenches around Chunuk Bair, 2001. *J. Griffiths*

Cape Helles have been designated war cemeteries and, as such, cannot be resumed for any other purpose. Only gradually is the land returning to its native state. In the meantime, you can still clamber into the remains of trenches, especially around Johnston's Jolly, or peer down deep tunnels. Until comparatively recently, the ground was dotted with rusted bully beef tins, battered old water bottles, spent cartridge cases and the like. A massive bushfire that swept through the peninsula in 1994 and, more recently, the fast-growing ranks of tourists have all but denuded the ground of its rusty relics. Nevertheless, a visitor today might still find an occasional item that has been washed to the surface by recent rains. The undergrowth is now thick and prickly, yet anyone who fights through it to explore more remote parts of the line may still see human bones scarring the surface as a chilling reminder of that carnage nearly nine decades ago.

For seventy-five years the Gallipoli battlefields were largely left undisturbed. But so great has become the flood of tourists in recent years, the Turkish government has had to build a new road just above the beach at Anzac Cove and create a special area north of the Cove to accommodate the thousands of Australians and New Zealanders who invade the peninsula for the Dawn Service on 25 April. When even these improvements could not accommodate the ever increasing numbers, the governments decided late in 2002 that, commencing in 2003, Anzac Day services at Gallipoli would

'Australians all let us rejoice for we are young and free . . .' These good-natured young revellers were part of the estimated 15 000 people who attended the dawn service at Anzac Cove, 25 April 2001. *Office of Australian War Graves*

henceforth be spread over two days: the traditional Australian and New Zealand services being held on 25 April and the Turkish international, French and Commonwealth services on 24 April. The antipodean tourists invariably bring along either their *Lonely Planet* guide or one of the several special Gallipoli books that have been produced by Australians in recent years. Local people give a broad smile and freely offer assistance when you mention the word 'Anzac'. It's hardly surprising—Australians and New Zealanders have transformed Gallipoli into a flourishing industry and the local Turks are happy to reap the profits.

For three years around the turn of the new century, historian Dr Bruce Scates surveyed Australians, young and old, who were making the pilgrimage to the Gallipoli peninsula. Prior to their visit, he reports, virtually all his respondents 'had no idea' of the scale of Turkish losses. 'Being in Turkey makes you realise that they were fighting for their country and in their country *we* were the enemy,' one Queenslander told him. Visiting the battlefields seems to truly bring home to people the common tragedy of war:

> The most moving experience was meeting Turkish people visiting their memorials . . . They would cry and pray and acknowledge their dead with such respect. We stayed one night on Chunuk Bair. Some friends and I went to watch the sun go down and . . . a family of Turkish people arrived. We moved out of their way so that they could take photos . . . but they wanted us to [stay] . . . One old woman took hold of my arm and was hugging me and crying . . . [A] young Turk . . . pointed to Rob and said 'You and me 80 years ago would be fighting but now we are friends . . . we respect you, Anzacs.' Here were these two young men shaking hands and smiling into the camera when they could have been fighting. It made me think—for what? Why did all those men die? Was it so Rob and the young Turk could stand today and be friends? I don't know.[24]

# A proud heritage

O ver 2500 years ago in central Asia, there lived a group of dispersed tribes loosely termed the Turkic people. Their name
came from the common language they spoke, a tongue somewhat
similar to Finnish, Hungarian and Estonian. Most of the tribes were
sheep-raising nomads who lived in tents called yurts, but some led a
settled life. In many respects they were quite an advanced civilisation,
knowing how to work iron and copper.

The lands and peoples of central Asia were, for centuries, under
the influence of the Chinese empires to the east and the Persian
empires in the west. History records a Persian invasion of central
Asia as early as the sixth century BC. It is thought that the famous
Great Wall of China was built to stop raids by the nomadic Turkic
and Mongolian tribes.

As time passed and the population grew, it became harder and
harder to eke out a satisfactory living from the lands of central Asia.
The nomadic tribes thus uprooted themselves and headed westward.
A significant movement took place during the fifth century AD when
Huns from Asia invaded Europe through lands north of the Caspian
Sea. They dislocated many Germanic tribes, caused the downfall of
the Western Roman Empire and established a short-lived state in
central eastern Europe. The Eastern Roman Empire (or Byzantine
Empire, as it was later called), with its capital in Constantinople,
weathered the invasion.

Another major migratory move by nomadic Turkic tribes
occurred in the eleventh century. This time the travellers journeyed
south of the Caspian Sea, then through Persia and Mesopotamia,

both of which were part of the Islamic Arab Empire. One of the largest of the migratory tribes, the Seljuks, managed to seize Baghdad, the capital of the empire, in 1055 and then advanced against the Christian Byzantine Empire. The Seljuks adopted Islam as their religion, then conducted a holy war against the infidel (non-Muslims). In 1071, at the Battle of Malazgirt (near Mount Ararat), the Seljuks defeated the Byzantine armies and began to occupy various Byzantine lands.

The move westward finally ended many decades later with the establishment of the Seljuk state in Anatolia (part of today's Turkey). Konya became its capital. Anatolia (meaning *east* in Greek), Asia Minor and Anadolu, which is the Turkish adaptation of Anatolia, are alternative names for the large area of land bounded by the Black Sea, the Aegean and Mediterranean. It has been the major route between Asia and Europe for hundreds of years. The famous Silk Road, for example, passed through it.

The Turks were not the first people to settle the region. Anatolia is thought to have been one of the cradles of Western civilisation. The Hittites of central Anatolia, for example, were possibly the first people to melt and cast copper and bronze. Many famous Greek colonies flourished on the Anatolian shores. Great city-states such as Ephesus, Pergamum and Troy were established here.

During the eleventh to thirteenth centuries, European Crusaders mounted repeated military campaigns in the Middle East and Anatolia. The Seljuks, wedged between the then-declining Islamic Arab and Christian Byzantine Empires, bore the brunt of many of the Crusaders' attacks. However, it was Mongols from the east rather than the Europeans who toppled the Seljuks in 1243 AD. After this conquest, the centralised Seljuk authority in Anatolia crumbled as various Turkish tribes established control over different parts of the land. The tribes fought among themselves and regularly raided nearby Byzantine settlements.

One such tribe, based near Constantinople, was led by a man named Osman. From this small group of people grew the mighty Ottoman Empire which, at its zenith in the seventeenth century, straddled the three continents around the Mediterranean Sea. They built a multi-ethnic, multicultural and multilingual empire based on military power consolidated through skilled diplomacy. The Ottomans or *Osmanlılar* (followers of Osman) regarded themselves more as Müslüman (the followers of Islam) than Turks.

The Ottomans drew substantially on the military skills of their Turkic past. The Turks were good, disciplined soldiers who were highly respected for these qualities. They were superb horsemen and mostly led simple lives. In summer, they led their flocks of sheep to rich highland pastures, then wintered on the warmer plains. The Islamic Arab Empire had recruited the Turks in great numbers as soldiers, and by the tenth century, most generals in the Arab Empire were of Turkish descent.

These military traditions were vigorously upheld for centuries by both the Turkish people and the Ottoman Empire. However, as the Empire expanded into Europe and as Ottoman armies were posted futher and further from their homeland, opposition from their families meant that it became increasingly difficult to maintain the traditional practice of drafting Turkish/Muslim boys into the army as cadets. To compensate for this shortfall, young Christian boys from conquered lands, frequently orphans, were engaged as army cadets and converted to Islam. This practice was both part of a conscious Islamicisation strategy as well as a convenient way of expanding the forces loyal to the sultans.

The Ottomans devised their own strategies of war and utilised many mercenaries and collaborators from other ethnic and religious backgrounds. They offered attractive incentives to induce foreigners to fight for them. All Christian recruits, for example, were exempted from paying taxes. The Ottoman armies were further strengthened through the practice of taking very young boys from conquered non-Muslim lands to be converted to Islam and trained in the sultan's army. The *yeniçeri* (new soldier), as he was called, daily learned and practised the art of war. He lived in special quarters near the palace and was forbidden to marry or own property. As compensation, he received high wages so the job was highly prized. Some families even gave bribes to ensure that their sons were drafted.

The Ottomans used a 'carrot and stick' approach to control other Muslim Turkish tribes. Conquered tribes were forced to pay annual taxes to the sultan (or *padişah*, the equivalent of a king or emperor) and provide troops whenever required. Conversely, those soldiers faithful to the empire were rewarded with plots of land. However, this land remained the property of the sultan and could be taken back or reallocated to somebody else at any time. This system enabled the sultans to forestall any internal challenges to their authority. Earlier rulers, whether they be Greek or Roman, had generally oppressed the Christian peasant farmers. When the Ottoman armies evicted these landlords, they lowered taxes. As the sultan was regarded as the ultimate owner of the land, the new Turkish/Islamic overlords were seen as merely caretakers of the land and its peasant population. This may explain why Ottoman rule generally was accepted quite well. For the peasant in the field, life became a little more bearable. However, all this changed from the seventeenth century onwards, as possibilities for further expansion diminished and the central government squeezed the peasants more and more for taxes and, later, for conscripts into the army.

Before being influenced by Muslim Arabs in the tenth century, the Turkish people were pagans who worshipped nature. Their conversion to Islam accelerated during the period of migration through Persia and Mesopotamia. Like many new converts, they soon became strong adherents and fought many holy wars against non-Muslims. The Islamic religion was founded by its prophet, Mohammed, early in the seventh century. Adherents of the faith must comply with five basic principles: they must accept Allah as the god and Mohammed as his prophet; they must pray five times each day; give alms to the poor; fast in the holy month of Ramadan; and, if possible, make a pilgrimage to the holy city of Mecca in Saudi Arabia. The *Koran* is the sacred book of Islam. Along with other religious codes, it forms the basics of Islamic law which governs all aspects of life. Many *yeniçeries* were reluctant converts, but the Ottomans developed appropriate strategies to persuade people to follow Islam. Extra taxes were levied on non-Muslims and those who accepted the faith and adopted a Muslim name were promoted or otherwise rewarded.

The beginning of the Ottoman Empire is dated to around 1300 AD when Osman established a small principality in the northwest of Anatolia. The Ottomans then began expanding into areas formerly controlled by the Byzantine Empire. In 1352, the Ottomans crossed into Europe via the straits of Gallipoli and started annexing territory in the Balkans.

The narrowness of this waterway had always made it an attractive passage between the two continents. As early as 480 BC, the Persian Emperor Xerxes crossed the Narrows to attack the Greek cities. The Persians constructed a bridge from boats and inflated animal skins, then reputedly transferred an army of half a million men from shore to shore in only seven days. Around 334 BC, the Macedonian king, Alexander the Great, with an army of 20 000 men, crossed the Narrows by boat at the beginning of a famous campaign that took him all the way to India.

By 1400, most of the Balkan lands were under Ottoman rule, and Constantinople was surrounded. Then a series of unexpected attacks by Mongols from the east put a stop, at least temporarily, to any further Ottoman expansion. Indeed, the emerging empire almost disintegrated. The Ottomans quickly reorganised, however, and after a brief period of internal turmoil, re-established their rule. The Byzantine capital, Constantinople, fell to them in 1453 and was renamed İstanbul.

The city was almost deserted when the conquerors moved in, but its population increased steadily and totalled nearly three quarters of a million people by the seventeenth century. İstanbul was home to many different ethnic and religious groups, all of which were allowed to control their own affairs and keep their language and traditions. As the capital of the Ottoman Empire, İstanbul established itself as a leading centre for trade and culture. Its cosmopolitan nature was probably meant to reflect the empire itself.

The straits of Çanakkale (Dardenelles) were always of the utmost importance to the Ottomans. Before they seized Constantinople, control of the straits was essential if the empire was to remain united. The waterway assumed an even greater strategic importance once İstanbul became the Ottoman capital. In 1463, two castles were built, one on either side of the straits, at Kilitbahir ('lock of the sea') in Europe, and Çanakkale in Asia. The forts guarded the narrowest point in the channel. The thirty cannons in each castle could fire cannon balls from one shore to the other, effectively sealing the straits.

Over the next two centuries, the Ottomans expanded their empire until it stretched from Vienna to Iran, and the Crimea to Yemen. The Mediterranean Sea was virtually an Ottoman lake! The empire reached its peak in the seventeenth century when any further expansion was deemed impracticable due to the extreme difficulty of conducting military campaigns along such extended supply lines. Also, the empire now bordered formidable new enemies such as Austria, Iran and Russia.

When the empire stopped expanding, the traditional sources of gaining extra revenue also dried up. This revenue was needed to satisfy an overblown administration and military, so the tax burden was shifted increasingly on to the peasants. These higher taxes no doubt caused discontent among the population. Also about this time, the English, Dutch and Portuguese took control of trade with India and thus deprived the Ottomans of another valuable revenue source. The economic downturn precipitated a general decline in the empire's fortunes. Things remained relatively stable throughout the seventeenth century, but territories were lost one after another in the two subsequent centuries. The slide began in earnest in 1683 when a large Ottoman army was routed at the gates of Vienna by a relief force comprising Polish forces and troops from a number of small Germanic fiefdoms that came to the aid of the Austrian Empire upon a call by the Pope to fight off the 'infidel Turks'.

As the cracks grew ever wider in the empire's façade, many attempts were made to reorganise the army and navy, the tax system and the bureaucracy. Nothing, however, succeeded in reversing the downward trend. The rise of powerful nation states such as France, England and Germany with their immensely increased capacity to produce goods cheaply due to the Industrial Revolution signalled the demise of an empire which still relied essentially on a feudal, non-mechanised pattern of production.

The European powers had, for many years, dreamed of carving up the rapidly declining Ottoman Empire. They could not agree, however, on how to divide up the spoils. Napoleon Bonaparte once remarked: 'The major question is who shall have İstanbul, not whether the Ottomans survive.' Whenever one power tried to acquire a chunk of the empire, the others invariably objected and

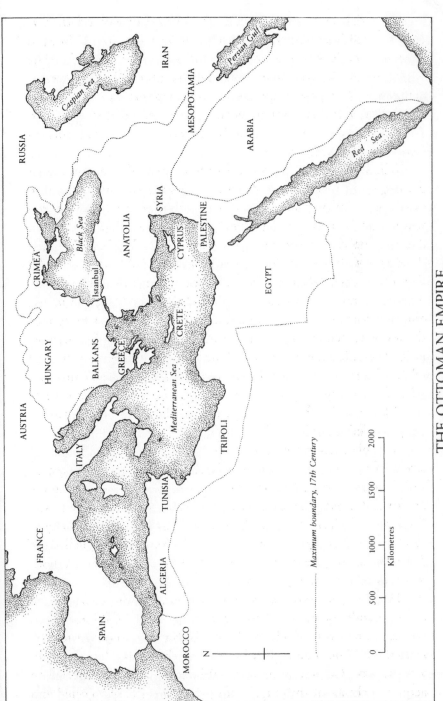

THE OTTOMAN EMPIRE

............. Maximum boundary, 17th Century

Kilometres

0    500    1000    1500    2000

threw their support behind the Ottomans. In the Crimean War of 1854–56, for example, the British and French joined with the Ottomans to stop Russia annexing Ottoman territory. A large fleet of British and French warships sailed through the Dardanelles and up the Bosphorus to attack Russian towns on the Black Sea coast.

In the decades following the French Revolution of 1789, the ideas of progress, freedom and popular nationalism began spreading into the western areas of the Ottoman Empire. Many ethnic groups began demanding their freedom, their cause invariably receiving the support of some or other of the great powers opposed to the Ottomans. This upsurge of nationalism and the consequent creation of many small new nations proved to be the straw that broke the camel's back, as the Ottomans lacked both the authority and the military power to arrest the trend.

By 1910, 'the sick man of Europe', as the empire was called, had lost most of its colonial territories. France had taken Algeria and Tunisia, the British occupied Egypt, and Italy had seized Tripoli. Then, during the Balkan wars of 1912–13, the Ottoman armies offered only six weeks of token resistance against Bulgarian, Greek and Serbian forces. At one stage, the border shrank almost to İstanbul itself.

It was about this time, largely as a reaction to the embarrassing losses and sacrifices that the Ottomans seemed constantly to be enduring, that an aggressive new political force emerged in İstanbul. Calling themselves the Young Turks, this group sought to replace the old Ottoman style multi-ethnic empire with an empire of Turks. The Young Turks appreciated only too well that the Ottomans (the rulers) of the empire had long since severed ties with their Turkish background in the belief that the Turkish peasant of Anatolia was neither cultured nor refined enough. The language of the sultan's court (*Osmanlıca*) had very little resemblance to the Turkish spoken in Anatolia. The nobles used so many words of Arabic and Persian origin that outsiders found it difficult to understand them! Moreover, the imperial court and government usually preferred to recruit people for high positions from its European dominions; even the sultan's mother was often of non-Turkish origin. The Young Turks sought to redress the scales in favour of the Turks.

The 'yenicheries' who, in earlier times were a driving force in expanding the empire, had gradually become more of an encumbrance than a help. Their voice became all-powerful in İstanbul; any sultan who ignored them put his own life at risk. Together with the religious establishment, the yenicheries constituted a formidable reactionary force. They thwarted any move to reorganise or modernise the army until many of their members were killed in the mutiny of 1826. The yenicheries were disbanded and, henceforth, the sultan conscripted most of his army from the Turkish/Muslim community. The training of this new army was entrusted largely to the Prussians (later the Germans). Cadets were also sent to France to learn the skills of modern warfare.

These cadets returned with other new ideas, too—the ideas of the French Revolution. The Young Turk movement grew out of this dissatisfaction. Years of failure on so many fronts had made people amenable to radical ideas. The new movement operated through an

The Golden Horn, İstanbul, 1919. The tall minarets of the mosques are still a prominent feature in the cityscape. *AWM G01783*

organisation called the Committee of Union and Progress. Its members were drawn mostly from the army and the emerging professional classes.

One prominent leader in the group was Enver, a battalion commander in Macedonia. He and his followers successfully led the committee in a struggle which resulted in the Young Turks gaining control in İstanbul (the 1908 Revolution). In 1909, they appointed a new sultan who, unlike his predecessors, was only a titular figurehead. A constitution, a parliament and a cabinet took the reins of the empire. These actions made the Young Turks very popular. However, in 1913, Enver and his Young Turks associates staged a *coup d'état*, displaced the parliament, installed a new sultan and took direct control. The new rulers tried to rejuvenate the old system by governing with an iron fist. Hundreds of old officers in the Ottoman army were retired overnight and the deposed sultan was kept under house arrest until his death in 1918. The government ruthlessly suppressed any opposition from minority groups within the empire, such as the Armenians.

Enver emerged as the truly strong man of the new administration and became virtually the uncrowned ruler of the Ottoman Empire. He was part of the ruling class with a lot of power and influence, having married the sultan's niece in 1913. He assumed the title Enver Paşa (*Paşa* roughly translates into English as General). Enver had spent some time in Germany as a military attaché and he greatly admired that nation's achievements. As his personal authority grew, so too the country's friendship with Germany flourished.

The Germans were very keen to cultivate Enver as a friend in the hope that it would yield them positive returns in trade and territory. In particular, the Germans sought control over the vast oil deposits that lay within the Ottoman lands. They were not the only ones at about this time to realise that oil was fast becoming an extremely valuable commodity and a great logistical weapon in wartime. The presence of oil in Mesopotamia (now Iraq) had been noted since ancient times. The classical Greek historian, Herodotus, for example, wrote of pitch (bitumen) being used as a binding agent in the walls of Babylon. German geologists had visited the area in 1871 and reported enthusiastically about natural seepages of oil.

The German Embassy, İstanbul, c.1914 with a group of Ottoman soldiers in the right foreground. *National Library of Australia*

In 1899, the Germans offered the Ottomans the financial capital and technical expertise to build a railway linking Berlin and Baghdad (capital of Mesopotamia). In return for their assistance, the Germans asked among other things that they be granted the mineral (including oil) rights twenty kilometres each side of the railway track. This offer aroused the suspicions of the Ottoman Government which subsequently learned of the oil deposits and rejected the German proposal. Curiously, however, no steps were then taken to exploit the oil.

Even before the turn of the century, oil companies were urging Britain's Royal Navy to convert its coal-powered ships to oil-fired engines. Senior naval officers readily accepted that oil-firing offered significant advantages over coal: increased speed, extended range, smokeless burning, improved manoeuvrability and more space aboard ship for armaments. Oil also meant easy refuelling at sea rather than always docking for coal loading. Britain, however, lacked any known deposits of oil and this factor alone convinced most that conversion would not be in the Royal Navy's best interests.

In 1911, Winston Churchill was appointed First Lord of the Admiralty. He was convinced that oil was the right fuel for the Navy, saying in an address to the British Parliament in July 1913: 'We must become the owners or at any rate the controllers at the source of at least a proportion of the supply of natural oil which we require.'[1] To achieve this goal, Churchill persuaded the British Government to buy two million pounds worth of shares in the Anglo Persian Oil Company. The parliamentary Act authorising the purchase received

Liman von Sanders, the German general who oversaw the re-organisation of the Ottoman Army in 1913. He subsequently commanded the Ottoman and German forces on Gallipoli in 1915. *AWM J00200*

its Royal Assent in late July 1914, less than a week before the Great War began.

Germany, in the meantime, was taking positive steps to further its links with the Young Turks. In December 1913, a German military mission headed by General Liman von Sanders arrived in İstanbul to reorganise the Ottoman Army. In a letter to his ambassador in İstanbul, the German Emperor wrote: 'Do not forget that I want to see Turks on my side. You may find good friends amongst young Turkish officers who were trained in Germany.'

Meanwhile, elsewhere in Europe, great imperialist powers were lining up against each other in two mighty alliances. On one side, Britain, France and Russia had combined in what was termed the Triple Entente; on the other, Germany and Austria–Hungary together constituted the Central Powers. The Ottomans sought to steer a middle course between these two massive power blocs by cultivating friendships with both sides. Several attempts were made to conclude a non-aggression pact with the Entente powers but all approaches failed. Britain rejected the Ottomans' overtures on three separate occasions. In late May 1914, the Young Turks went to Russia in search of a suitable pact but once again made no headway.

On 28 June 1914 the Austrian Archduke Franz Ferdinand and his wife were assassinated in Sarajevo, Serbia. Austria held Serbia responsible for the murders and issued an ultimatum to the Serbian government on 23 July. Russia resented Austria's strident demands and stood by its ally, Serbia. Over the next few days, the complex web of alliances rapidly drew all the great European powers into war.

Enver Paşa signed a secret alliance with Germany on 2 August 1914, the day after the Central Powers had declared war on Russia. By 4 August, a general state of war existed between the Entente and the Central Powers. Enver Paşa had, for the moment, kept his country out of the war. His pact with Germany ensured that he had a powerful ally if any other nation attacked them. By the same token, the pact also threatened to draw the Ottomans into the new European battlefields.

Mustafa Kemal, an able young officer and an important member of the Young Turks movement, was only one of many members of the Committee of Union and Progress who opposed the alliance with

PUNCH, OR THE LONDON CHARIVARI.—November 11, 1914.

HIS MASTER'S VOICE.

THE KAISER (*to Turkey, reassuringly*). "LEAVE EVERYTHING TO ME, ALL YOU'VE GOT TO DO IS TO EXPLODE."
TURKEY. "YES, I QUITE SEE THAT. BUT WHERE SHALL *I* BE WHEN IT'S ALL OVER?"

This cartoon from the English magazine, *Punch*, 11 November 1914, typifies the Allied view that the Ottoman government was a mere puppet of the German Kaiser.

Germany. Their reasoning was simple: if Germany loses, the Ottoman Empire is finished; if she wins, the empire merely becomes her satellite.

Enver Paşa curtly dismissed these reservations. He could hear the drums of war approaching, and hoped they might recapture past glories and lost territories. A string of coincidences made it just that bit easier for Enver to take the Ottoman Empire into the war. The empire's navy had very close links with Britain; British officers held key positions and two new warships were being built in Britain. The ships had been paid for by public donations; indeed, the money had already been handed over to the British. On the eve of the outbreak of war, just as the ships were nearing completion, Britain requisitioned them for her own defensive needs. Not surprisingly, this turned Turkish public opinion very much against Britain. On 9 August 1914, soon after this incident, Enver allowed two German warships stranded in the Mediterranean to escape from the British Navy by entering the Dardanelles Straits. The German Government subsequently sold them to the Ottomans to replace the ships Britain had withheld. One of the terms of the sale was that German officers should replace the British advisers within the navy. Later, a German admiral was officially installed as Commander-in-Chief of the Ottoman Navy and received a hero's welcome in İstanbul.

Germany was very keen to have the Ottomans with them in the war. With the help of Enver Paşa, who was now the leader of the Committee of Union and Progress. Minister of War, Chief of the General Staff, and groom to the sultan, the empire's neutrality was quickly eroded. On Enver's secret orders, the Imperial Navy, including the two new German warships, sailed into the Black Sea in late October

Ottoman troops in training, late 1914. *BBC Hulton Picture Library*

1914. It shelled some Russian coastal towns and sank several Russian ships. The attacks brought the two countries to the brink of war. This suited Germany admirably, as war between Russia and the Ottomans would relieve some of the pressure facing her forces in the east.

Russia, France and Britain delivered a twelve-hour ultimatum to the Ottoman rulers as soon as they heard of the Black Sea attacks. Enver did not issue any response, so hostilities formally began the next day, 31 October. The Ottoman Empire entered the war with a population of over twenty million people, half of whom were Turkish. A general mobilisation had been ordered some months earlier, thus the nation was not wholly unprepared for war. Many Turks, then and now, refer to World War I as *Seferberlik* (mobilisation).

After the declaration of war, Enver Paşa and his deputies embarked on two catastrophic military campaigns: one in the east against Russia and the other against the British in the Suez Canal area. The Russian campaign commenced in mid-winter with an ill-prepared army of 90 000 men. Enver led the contingent, even though he had only limited experience as a commander in the field. He soon led the army to its death—thousands of troops died on the battlefield but even more succumbed to the intense cold. Enver's blind following of the Germans' advice had caused terrible loss of life; the Ottomans' casualties were estimated to total 75 000 men.

Enver's other offensive aimed to seize Egypt from the British or, failing that, at least prevent shipping from passing through the Suez Canal. He despatched a rag-tag army of 16 000 men into Egypt but it proved incapable of forcing its way over the Canal. After losing about a thousand men in the campaign, the Ottoman Army turned for home. Little did it know that, in a matter of a few weeks, many of the Allied troops it had encountered in Egypt would be spearheading an invasion of Gallipoli.

The British force in Egypt included 20 000 Australian and 8000 New Zealand troops recently arrived from their southern homelands. The Australian and New Zealand Army Corps, soon abbreviated to ANZAC, had expected to be shipped directly to Europe and there join other British and Dominion armies on the Western Front. But soon after the troopships left Australia, the British authorities diverted the convoy to Egypt. The Anzacs were hugely disappointed; they had joined up to fight the dreaded Hun and it now seemed they might not get their chance to win fame and glory on the battlefield.

Why, you might ask, should Australians and New Zealanders be joining in a European war brought on by the assassination of an obscure Austrian archduke in the Bosnian city of Sarajevo? After all, Sarajevo was thousands of miles away and few Australians had any link with the Austro–Hungarian Empire or the Balkans. Probably the only immediate interest in the event for Australia was that the unfortunate duke had once visited Sydney aboard an Austrian warship. But, viewed in 1914's terms, the realities were very different from how we might see them today. Australia and New Zealand were both members of the British Empire and maintained close links with 'mother' England. Only a century and a quarter earlier, British people had first migrated to the great southern lands, dispossessing the long-time owners, the Aborigines.

Australia had gained the status of a nation in 1901 when the six colonies combined to form the Commonwealth of Australia. In many respects, this political independence was a misnomer since many Australians, especially the wealthy and those in high places, still relied heavily on Britain as their mentor and chief source of inspiration. Britain's trials and triumphs were seen as Australia's, too. Thus, the Australian colonies had quickly despatched military contingents to help fight Britain's wars in Sudan, in South Africa and in China.

It was not surprising, therefore, that when Archduke Ferdinand's assassination rapidly exploded into a major international crisis threatening to engulf all Europe in war, most Australians responded enthusiastically. The prime ministers of both Australia and New Zealand offered their troops to Britain even before war had been declared. The patriotism of the empire swelled in many a breast. Students at Melbourne University, for example, concluded their lectures on 2 August by standing to sing the national anthem. Throughout the next few days, large crowds milled around newspaper offices awaiting the latest news. The tension finally broke at 12.30 p.m. on 5 August when the local press announced that Britain was at war with Germany. 'Some [among the crowd] were enthusiastic, some evidently gratified; some seemed overweighted by the impact of the news, some were openly pessimistic', reported next day's Melbourne *Argus*, 'but the general feeling was one of relief that the terrible waiting and uncertainty of the last few days was over . . .'.

The news was greeted in most quarters with enthusiasm. A few voices questioned the wisdom of war but most people were swept along by the razzle-dazzle and rhetoric of the occasion—the crowds, the flags, the bands and the stirring speeches. People wanted to feel involved; they even wanted to feel threatened. Thus sentries were posted to guard bridges and railway lines in the belief, perhaps the hope, the Germans might somehow attack them.

A human avalanche descended upon the recruiting stations immediately the doors were opened. Ten thousand men enlisted in Sydney in little over a week. 'Great wars were rare, and short, and many eagerly seized a fleeting opportunity', comments Australian historian Bill Gammage.[2] Those who got accepted considered themselves

Early recruits drilling at the Blackboy Hill training camp near Perth, Western Australia. Only one man (other than the officer) wearing any semblance of a military uniform and most seem more interested in the camera than the drill sergeant! *AWM A03404*

lucky. War was glamorous, soldiering romantic and death glorious but unlikely.

It was not long before the local papers were reprinting stories from England of Germany's alleged barbarity—bayoneting babies, raping and killing women, severing prisoners' hands, and a host of similar fabrications. Knowing no better, Australians readily accepted the stories. Largely in response to these stories, many Australians instantly turned against anyone and anything around them remotely German in origin. People with German names were attacked or hounded, German businesses boycotted and ludicrous gestures made such as renaming 'strasburg sausage' 'Belgian sausage' in honour of the country first invaded by the Boche. The St Kilda Football Club felt so embarrassed at accidentally having team colours which matched the German flag that its players pinned Union Jacks to their jumpers. Before the next season began, the club changed from red, black and yellow to red, black and white.

Initially, the hate propaganda was all directed against Germany and German descendants. Very few Turks resided in Australia and Australians knew little about the Ottoman Empire. What knowledge they did possess was highly simplistic. Thus, an Australian primary school textbook written in 1899 described the Turks as 'a cruel and ignorant race ... one of the most fanatical of the Mohammedan races', the ferocity of the 'unspeakable Turk' in gaining converts being unsurpassed by any other race.[3] The Ottomans' entrance into the war was seen in Britain and Australia as proof that it was a pawn of Germany, a second- (or third-) rate nation lacking the capacity for independent action. This analysis totally overlooked any similarities with Australia's position vis-à-vis Britain.

Australia's war with the Ottoman Empire first became a reality through a strange series of events in Broken Hill, New South Wales, on New Year's Day, 1915. That morning a thousand local holiday-makers set out on a picnic train for nearby Silverton. The holiday mood was abruptly shattered when two 'Turks' opened fire on the train, killing three picnickers and wounding several others. Another man was shot as the assailants tried to escape. They were soon cornered and shot by local police.

Both men were, in fact, Afghans, not Turks. One was an elderly camel driver, the other a miner who had spent some years in the Ottoman Army. The author of a history of Broken Hill, Brian Kennedy, has concluded that '[a]pparently they decided on their suicidal mission out of a mixture of religious zeal, resentment at past slights, and loyalty to the Sultan; it is also probable that they were under the influence of "bhang" at the time'.[4]

Local reaction was swift and savage. About a thousand people, mainly young men, gathered in the main street that evening and marched on the town's German club, singing 'Rule Britannia' as they broke in and set it alight. Groups then made off for the Afghan camp several miles out of town, but a force of sixty police and infantry prevented them attacking the camp's inhabitants. The angry mob gradually dispersed.

The incident made headlines across Australia. It seemed to confirm earlier warnings from the government and others that the war might very soon reach Australia. News of the attack must have rankled with the Anzacs who were still biding their time in Egypt. More action could be had in outback New South Wales, it seemed, than overseas with the Australian Imperial Force! The soldiers need not have worried; their time would come soon enough.

# THREE

# *Defending the homeland*

As you sit at one of the many quayside restaurants of Çanakkale sipping your *çay* (Turkish tea), great ships glide past you like ducks in a funfair shooting gallery. With binoculars you can easily see people moving about on the decks. The waterway is aptly named 'The Narrows' for less than 1500 metres separate Çanakkale from the other shore. This thin stretch of sea is but the narrowest section of the Dardanelles Straits, a 66-kilometre blue thread that divides Europe and Asia. Your restaurant table is in Asia, yet, as you gaze across the Narrows, you stare into Europe. The ship you watch is perhaps only 800 metres away. If it is steaming up the straits towards İstanbul, it must advance against the strong current sweeping down from the Sea of Marmara to the Aegean. An even better view of the ship can be obtained from the European side where rugged, barren cliffs rise up practically out of the sea to provide panoramic views up and down the waterway. These three factors—the narrowness of the waterway, the strong south-flowing current and the rugged European coastline—make the Dardanelles a formidable natural barrier at the southern gateway to Turkey.

This waterway has for centuries been seen by foreigners as the door through which Anatolia could be invaded and conquered. Generations of Turks had built a series of defences to make sure the door remained firmly shut. By 1914, these defences were a strange assortment of the old and the new. The entrance to the straits was guarded by four forts, two on each shore, with massive stone walls built up to 250 years earlier by Ottoman sultans anxious to keep out unwanted ships. Seventeen kilometres up the straits was another series of forts

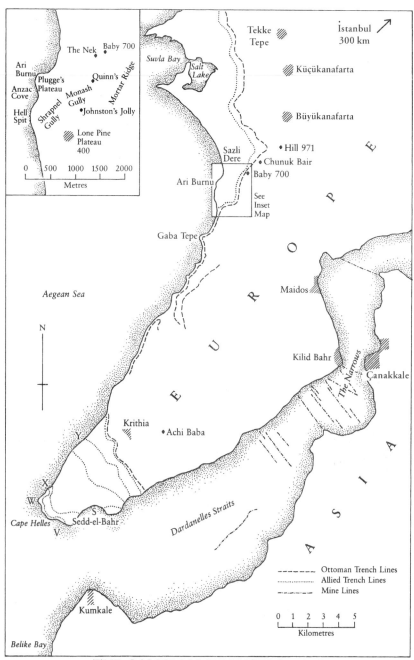

The Nek • Baby 700
Ari Burnu
Plugge's Plateau
Anzac Cove
Monash Gully
Quinn's
Mortar Ridge
Shrapnel Gully
Hell Spit
• Johnston's Jolly
Lone Pine
Plateau
400

0  500  1000  1500  2000
Metres

Tekke Tepe
İstanbul
300 km
Suvla Bay
Salt Lake
Küçükanafarta
Büyükanafarta
• Hill 971
• Chunuk Bair
Baby 700
Sazli Dere
Ari Burnu
See Inset Map
Gaba Tepe

Aegean Sea

N

E U R O P E

Maidos
Kilid Bahr
The Narrows
Çanakkale

Krithia
• Achi Baba

A S I A

Y
X
W
S
Sedd-el-Bahr
Cape Helles
V
Dardanelles Straits

Kumkale

Belike Bay

- - - - - Ottoman Trench Lines
.......... Allied Trench Lines
- · - · - Mine Lines

0  1  2  3  4  5
Kilometres

## THE GALLIPOLI PENINSULA, 1915

50

and a single line of sea mines shore to shore. Then, at the Narrows, was the third and most formidable line of defence. No less than eleven forts (five on the European shore, six in Asia) guarded the sea lane. The shorelines were dominated by two huge white stone fortresses built by the Ottomans in the fifteenth century. In all, there were over 100 heavy- and medium-calibre guns positioned along the straits, but only fourteen of these were modern long-range weapons. Moreover, as the official Turkish account of the Dardanelles campaign later admitted: 'Not only were the majority of the guns of old pattern, with a slow rate of fire and short range, but their ammunition supply was also limited.'[1] In short, the defence system was far more brittle than its outward appearance suggested.

When war broke out in August 1914, the Ottomans immediately began improving the Dardanelles defences. A German general was co-opted to advise and assist the fortress commander and new minefields were laid. The arrival of an Allied fleet outside the straits

Outside the Çanakkale military museum a 1914 torpedo-firing tube still guards the Narrows. On the far shore, a large memorial etched into the hillside reminds ferry passengers crossing between Çanakkale and Eceabat of the many men who died on Gallipoli. *H. H. Başarın*

added a new sense of urgency to the task. Three days after Britain declared war on the Ottoman Empire, Allied ships briefly shelled the outermost Dardanelles forts. Two lucky shots during the twenty-minute bombardment put the shore guns out of action. This lulled British and French gunners into believing they could easily reduce all the forts to rubble. For the defenders, the attack was a timely lesson. 'The bombardment of 3 November warned me', the forts commander wrote later, 'and I realised that I must spend the rest of my time in developing the defences by every means.'[2]

The damaged forts were soon repaired. In addition, new heavy guns and searchlights were installed, mobile howitzers introduced, more mines laid, and three torpedo-firing tubes were mounted in the Narrows. Undoubtedly, the key defensive component was the line of mines approaching the Narrows (see map page 50). By early March 1915, over 350 mines had been laid in a geometric pattern that gave large warships only a one-in-a-hundred chance of passing through unscathed. The Allies had minesweeping trawlers but they were very slow. Their speed was further reduced by the strong current, so the Ottoman gunners could make things very hot for the invading navy.

Spurred on by the successful November bombardment and frustrated with the trench stalemate of the Western Front, the British war lords resolved in late January 1915 to launch a major naval assault against the Dardanelles. Once the straits were conquered, they predicted, the Ottoman rulers would quickly surrender rather than see İstanbul bombarded. Britain despatched the *Queen Elizabeth*, the largest battleship in the world, to lead the attack.

The assault opened on 19 February with the long-range bombardment of the outer forts. Nine ships engaged the forts for nearly eight hours but inflicted little real damage. Bad weather then intervened and the attack was not resumed until 25 February. This time the battleships scored many direct hits. The forts were practically destroyed and their soldiers forced to withdraw. The way was now clear for the Allied fleet to enter the straits and attack the next line of forts. In İstanbul, preparations were made to evacuate the sultan, his court, the Treasury and the leading military and civilian authorities. Confidence was so high within Britain's War Council that papers were circulated discussing what peace terms might be offered to the Ottomans. Small forces of British marines were put ashore on 26 February to destroy more guns. The parties failed to achieve their goal as the Ottoman troops put up stout defence and inflicted considerable casualties on the raiders.

The British tried a fresh approach on 5 March. The *Queen Elizabeth* was sent up the peninsula and anchored off Gaba Tepe. Her massive guns then fired over the peninsula peaks and on to the forts along the Narrows. The Ottomans were powerless to reply. The fort walls at Çanakkale today still bear the scars of the bombardment. A gun was rushed to Gaba Tepe that night, forcing the British ship further offshore, thereby greatly reducing the accuracy of its fire. Meanwhile, British minesweepers operating inside the straits were enjoying little success; the slow trawlers could barely make headway against the current and thus became virtual stationary targets for the shore guns.

Ottoman morale soared as the British and French ships struggled to subdue the defenders. The level of resistance seemed to be increasing almost daily. An American naval historian has written of this phase in the campaign:

> The Turks were [now] alert and constantly increased the effectiveness of the [artillery] batteries by building more emplacements, increasing the roads and trails over which the guns were moved, and repeatedly shifting the batteries. The Turks were short of ammunition and did not indulge in firing unless the target was tempting and usually a gun or battery did not return the fire but relied upon a neighbouring battery to punish the attacking vessels ... Actual damage to the ships ... was small but the defence was increasing in efficiency and the [Ottoman] howitzers were always a menace due to their plunging fire.[3]

The British admiral commanding the fleet decided it was time to launch an all-out attack. The battle began at 10.45 a.m. on 18 March. Eighteen battleships and a bevy of cruisers and destroyers moved within close range of the shore guns. Simultaneously, trawlers commenced sweeping the minefields. Coincidentally, an Ottoman minelayer, the *Nusret*, had laid twenty-six new mines the previous night. At first the attack went well for the Allies. The German *Official History* comments:

An amazing artillery battle began . . . It appeared beyond human capability to tolerate this hell; but nonetheless, the Turks and Germans stayed and did their duty. Behind the hills, flashes and flames were raging and the air was filled with cracking noises. Red flashes were visible through the clouds of smoke and columns of earth that had been whipped-up by the bombardment from the big guns.[4]

During the 18 March battle, this Ottoman artilleryman, Corporal Seyyit, performed the prodigiuous feat of lifting 258 kilogram shells by hand after the gun's loading mechanism jammed at one of Dardanelles forts. Later he was asked to demonstrate how he'd done it but, without the adrenalin rush of combat, he could not repeat the feat, and so a dummy shell was used for the photographer. *AWM A05301*

The forts were silenced by noon but then a French ship hit a mine and sank. Then two more battleships were hit and sunk and another three crippled. The minesweepers fared even worse and fled in disorder. By late afternoon, one third of the fleet had been sunk or put out of action, yet no ship had even reached the Narrows. The ships swung around in retreat.

Naturally, the Ottomans were jubilant. They had repulsed the greatest naval power in the world yet had lost only forty-four men killed (including eighteen Germans) and seventy-four wounded. Seven hundred Allied sailors had perished. The shore guns had that day fired an enormous amount of ammunition. In British post-war mythology it is sometimes claimed that the fleet retired just as the Ottoman ammunition supply expired, but recent research has revealed that enough shells were on hand to repulse another two attacks. Besides, it was mines rather than guns that inflicted most of the damage.

The victory was the Ottoman Empire's first for many, many years. Thus, the achievement was of immense psychological as well as military value. As mentioned in chapter one, the occasion is still commemorated each year by Turks. On both sides of the straits, massive memorials remind travellers of the momentous event. The old fort at Çanakkale has been converted into a museum and the *Nusret*, built in Germany in 1913, stands in dry dock open for public inspection. Local tourist shops sell large colour posters of the Allied ships exploding. In many respects, 18 March is to Turks what 25 April is to Australians and New Zealanders: the day on which their small force courageously overcame apparently daunting military odds to secure an heroic, if temporary, victory.

An interested spectator at the 18 March debacle was the English general, Sir Ian Hamilton, who had arrived only twenty-four hours earlier to take command of any commitment the army might be required to make. In his mind, the stout Ottoman defence displayed on 18 March justified the British rethinking their strategy. He telegraphed Lord Kitchener back in London:

> I am being most reluctantly driven to the conclusion that the Straits are not likely to be forced by battleships, as at one time seemed probable, and that if

my troops are to take part, it will not take the subsidiary form anticipated. The Army's part will be more than mere landing parties to destroy forts; it must be a deliberate and prepared operation, carried out at full strength, so as to open a passage for the Navy.[5]

In essence, Hamilton was recommending that the army now be given its chance to lead the assault. Britain's leaders concurred with his judgment. Before the month was out, Hamilton had moved to Alexandria and was planning his attack.

A similar strategic reappraisal was undertaken by the Ottomans. Following the 18 March victory, Enver Paşa ordered his senior German adviser, General Liman von Sanders, to take command of the forces at the Dardanelles. Von Sanders had been sent from Germany to reorganise the Ottoman Army but clearly the Dardanelles emergency was now of far more pressing importance. His new appointment represented a total about-face in Ottoman military planning. When the war began, Enver had insisted that national defence be divided into two parts: one command in Asia, the other in Europe. Von Sanders's new post acknowledged that it made much more sense to divide the country into north and south rather than east and west. Von Sanders and his fifth Army would be responsible for defending both the European and Asian approaches to the straits.

The German general left İstanbul the very day, 26 March, that Hamilton set off for Egypt to muster his forces. Von Sanders set up his headquarters in what had been the French consular agent's house in the small town of Gelibolu (Gallipoli). This pretty harbourside town on the Sea of Marmara takes its name from a Greek word meaning *nice town*. Most of his staff officers were Ottoman, but Germans filled a number of key command and technical positions. This caused many problems as few of the Ottomans spoke German and even fewer Germans understood Turkish. Thus von Sanders's map of the Arafartalar sector had each feature marked in Ottoman Arabic script with a phonetic translation handwritten beneath. Similar language problems existed for the British and French, although many well-educated English people studied French at school and vice versa.

With language being such a stumbling block, the interpreter became a key figure at many command posts. One German officer who fought at Gallipoli said he was like a deaf and dumb person and had to rely totally on his interpreter as a go-between. It was a frustrating experience as his interpreter had an incomplete grasp of German and thus often did not comprehend the real meaning of his orders. Other cultural differences only worsened the confusion, as the German officer relates:

> There are so many opportunities for misunderstandings, quite apart from the mistakes made in translations by the interpreters, as for example in the rather important definition of clocktime: 6 a.m. according to the German is 6 in the morning, that is 6 hours after midnight, whether it is dark or light; but 6 a.m. according to the Turk is 6 hours after sunrise, which, as everybody knows, varies all the time.
>
> The designation of the days is different too, for the calendar of the Moslems begins with the flight of the Prophet from Mecca to Medina . . . [for example, 19 May 1915 is the Muslim 6 May 1331].[6]

Faced with such difficulties, it seems something of a minor miracle that any coordinated defence was mounted, let alone one that proved itself so effective.

The partnership undoubtedly had its problems, but officers from both countries speak warmly of their ally. A German colonel, for example, wrote after the war:

> The German–Turkish brotherhood in arms on Gallipoli was highly successful and bore fruit. Of course conflicts occurred. But where would that not have been the case during a campaign, when opinions clash harshly and time urges for action? I believe that on Gallipoli such conflicts were fewer than otherwise the case in armies with a nationally homogeneous corps of officers.[7]

This loyalty to the alliance was also shared by the Ottomans. When an Australian historical mission visited Gallipoli immediately after the war, an Ottoman colonel toured the old battlefields with them. One night at the mess table, an Australian thoughtlessly made a disparaging comment about Germany's war effort. The Ottoman colonel instantly replied: 'I think these people made a wonderful effort against their many opponents.'[8]

In deciding how best to defend the coastline, von Sanders had to guess what Hamilton would do. Given the forces and ships available, where would he land? What points along the coast offered the best places to put troops ashore? Which points would be hardest for the Ottomans to defend? Would Hamilton favour an all-out assault on one beach or a coordinated series of landings along the coast? The number of troops available to von Sanders was strictly limited as many units were still needed on the Russian front so it was literally of life-and-death importance that he guessed right.

Von Sanders was told on his arrival at Gelibolu that the Ottoman troops were spread along the coastline. This he condemned as wasteful and dangerous. He decided the Asiatic coast seemed the most vulnerable point and consequently posted two divisions (approximately 22 000 men) near Troy. Another two divisions were despatched north to Bulair. A fifth division was sent to Cape Helles while the sixth and final division was ordered to Maidos (now Eceabat), a small town on the Narrows. Led by Lieutenant-Colonel Mustafa Kemal, this division had a roving commission. Maidos was centrally located, hence the troops there could be quickly despatched to reinforce whichever front proved decisive.

Even before von Sanders took command, Ottoman troops on the peninsula had begun systematically to improve their defensive position. Trenches were dug overlooking likely landing points and barbed wire or other barricades were stretched across the shallows near the beaches. In many instances, tools and equipment were in short supply so the fences of gardens and fields were stripped of wood and wire. All this work was done at night so as not to alert the enemy. The scheme did not fool the British, but it certainly worried them. A senior British naval officer, Admiral de Robeck, told Hamilton that 'not one living soul has been seen, since the engagement of our marines at the end of February, although each morning brings forth fresh evidence of nocturnal activity'.[9]

The defence program quickened considerably once von Sanders had taken stock of the position. Local communications were primitive, with few roads being fit for motor cars. As speed and flexibility were likely to be crucial, von Sanders ordered that new roads and bridges be commenced immediately. He also had new landing stages erected to improve communications across the Narrows. Extra supply dumps were laid and field bakeries built. In addition, the

Ottoman troops in training on cliffs along the Gallipoli Peninsula. *AWM H13571*

troops were given instruction in hand grenade throwing and sniping. All the programs were aimed at improving the mobility and adaptability of the Ottoman force. The state of preparedness was, nevertheless, far from perfect. Most roads were still mere tracks, there were no railways, and local telegraph and telephone systems were rudimentary. The German *Official History* of the campaign remarks that 'everything had to be done with too few workers who had insufficient training and tools. Therefore, the amount of work accomplished bore no comparison to what might have been done'.[10] The deficiencies in the Ottoman defence system meant that a well-devised attack might still be able to surprise the defenders.

The Allies greatly overestimated their capacity to effect a surprise landing. It was well known that Hamilton was about to attempt a massive invasion of the Gallipoli peninsula. From early April, British and French ships loaded with troops and supplies converged on the Greek island of Lemnos, eighty kilometres from the entrance to the straits. The invasion plan was perhaps the worst-kept secret of the entire war, although it has to be admitted that hiding 'one of the greatest maritime spectacles of the war' was asking a great deal of any admiral. Ottoman agents in Egypt and on Lemnos soon reported that the Allied force would consist of 50 000 British, Indian, Australian and New Zealand troops under General Hamilton and 30 000 French troops under General d'Amade. By 20 April, more than 200 ships were assembled in the island's harbour ready to take the troops to the beaches of Gallipoli. Censorship was so lax that reports of the imminent assault had even filtered back to Australia.

What the defenders did not know was exactly when and where the landings would occur. Hamilton had planned a multi-pronged attack. Australian troops would be rowed ashore at first light on the beaches near Gaba Tepe. The men would go ashore without any accompanying naval bombardment so as to maximise the chances of surprise. Soon after these men were landed, warships would blast Cape Helles, then British troops would land at five beaches around the toe of the peninsula. If all went to plan, the Anzacs would sweep eastward to Maidos and the Narrows as the British advanced up from the south. To further confuse the defenders, diversionary feint attacks were planned for Bulair (in the north) and across the straits at Belike Bay and Kum Kale in Asia Minor. All in all, 75 000 Allied troops were being pitted against 84 000 Ottomans. The landing day was scheduled to be 23 April, but bad weather forced its postponement to 25 April.

As the days passed, the Allied troops repeatedly practised jumping from the boats as they would at the real landings. Most of them had little real idea what lay ahead. Many had never before even heard of Gallipoli and knew equally little about the Ottomans and the Turks. One British major recalls he:

> ... had visions of trekking up the Gallipoli peninsula with the Navy bombarding the way for us up the straits and along the coastline of the sea of Marmosa [sic], until after a brief campaign we enter triumphantly Constantinople, there to meet the Russian Army, which would link up with ourselves to form part of a great chain encircling and throttling the central Empires. I sailed from England on 20 March, 1915, firmly convinced that my vision would actually come true and that some time in

1915 the paper-boys would be singing out in the streets of London: 'Fall of Constantinople—British link hands with Russians'.[11]

But even a brief look at the terrain was enough to warn most soldiers that this would be no easy victory. Joseph Murray, a British private, was aboard ship off the peninsula the day after the great battle of 18 March. 'As we steamed slowly down the western coast of the Gallipoli Peninsula', he wrote in his diary, 'we were ordered to man the rails in full battle order, which we did, our bayonets glistening in the sun . . . In full view of the Turks, we expected the order to disembark at any moment but the order was not given this day. For two hours we remained on view, watching and wondering. No doubt the Turks were also wondering exactly where and when we would strike; as invaders it was for us to choose the time and place . . . The Turks had to remain where they were, ready to defend their homeland.'[12]

Private Murray was perhaps unusual in that he admitted to being an invader. The overwhelming majority of the Allied troops and even many history books have suggested that the attackers were a liberating force coming to teach the Ottomans a lesson or rescue them from their German overlords. This view is quite mistaken. As Murray says, the Allies were about to invade the Ottoman Empire and hoped to change its government by force of arms. Often, in the days leading up to the landing, Murray pondered the senselessness of war. He wondered, for example, if it would be wisest to kill the wounded rather than leave them behind. 'Perhaps the rules of war, which I did not even pretend to know, allow humans to suffer. People are inclined to turn a blind eye on individual suffering, especially if the suffering is out of sight. Maybe some day when war is brought to everyone's doorstep then, and only then, will the peoples of the world wake up to the folly of mass slaughter as a means of settling international disputes.'[13] It was comparatively easy and certainly quite painless for politicians and generals, whether they be in London, Paris, Melbourne or İstanbul, to send troops off to war. Things were not so simple for the common soldier. Even before he had entered battle, Murray had realised that war was seldom glorious and never bloodless. Perhaps, too, he already knew that the

Ottomans would, in all probability, fight with great ferocity as they were defending their homeland against the invading 'infidels'.

Matters were now fast reaching a climax. Liman von Sanders was acutely aware of the danger in overcommitting his forces by deploying too many men to guard the coastline. If all units were deployed yet somehow the enemy still broke through, all would be lost. Thus, only small detachments, usually a company of 200 men, were stationed at possible landing sites. Most of his troops were quartered a little inland, ready to move into action wherever a major threat materialised. Spring had arrived; the *Official German History* notes 'the clay coloured hills, burnt by last summer's sun, now shimmered in the most beautiful greens; countless flowers were a delight to the eye. The air, wonderfully clear, brought everything nearer; one could almost touch the peaks and the beautiful rolling hills of Tenedos, Imbros and Samothrace. The vivid blue sea lay calm . . . .'.[14]

For the men guarding the beaches, the night of 24 April must have seemed much as any other night. The weather was improving and the sea seemed 'as smooth as satin'. It was a 'gloriously cool, peaceful night'.[15] Once the moon set at 3 a.m. everything was intensely dark until, about an hour later, the first tinges of the grey dawn appeared behind the hills. Every now and then a searchlight lazily perused the straits. All along the coast, Ottoman sentries peered seaward for signs of anything unusual. Most were probably half asleep, in spite of the chill morning air. Then, at 4.29 a.m. a sentry just south of Arı Burnu point saw a flare of flame and sparks lasting thirty seconds or so. It was the funnel of a small steamboat towing three landing craft crammed with Australian troops. Immediately, the sentry flashed a signal to the trench overlooking the point. There, a soldier jumped up and saw thirty-six rowboats just offshore. He shouted to his mates who shook themselves into action. After some seconds of disbelief, they fired a few shots. This quickly grew into a steady stream of bullets. The lead made sparks on the shingle beach as the first boats grounded in the shallows.

The Australians leapt from their boats into the water. A few found it deeper than they thought and were dragged under by their heavy packs and drowned. Others were hit, but most waded ashore, ran across the narrow beach, then sheltered under the sandy bank of a cliff which ran down to the beach. A few defenders were seen to run inland as the Australians scrambled up the steep gravel cliffs. The Anzacs had been told not to shoot until daylight, but many were returning the enemy fire. Already, bayonet and bullet were claiming Ottoman and Australian lives. By 4.40 a.m. an Ottoman gun behind Gaba Tepe (three kilometres south of Arı Burnu) was shelling the troop ships standing offshore. So began one of the largest amphibious landing assaults ever attempted in military history.

Seventy years later, an Australian television crew interviewed one of the last surviving Ottoman veterans who had witnessed the first Australian landings. Adil Şahin was a 16-year-old shepherd from the small village of Büyük Anafarta on the Gallipoli peninsula when he and thirty-two other men from his village were recruited into the 27th Battalion of the fifth Ottoman Army. Adil recounted for the Australian television cameras how just before dawn on 25 April, he had been asleep in a shallow trench with other riflemen just above the beach at the southern end of Anzac Cove when the duty sentry awakened them urgently.

'He shook us and pointed down the slope to the water below', Adil said. 'He said he thought he could see shapes out there on the water. We looked out and strained to see in the half-light and then we heard noises and saw shapes of boats with soldiers coming ashore. We were ordered to start firing. Some fell on the beach and I wasn't sure whether we'd hit them or they were taking shelter. They made for the base of the rise and then began climbing. We were outnumbered, so we began to withdraw.'[16] Adil did not find out until much later that the soldiers were Australians.

'It was very confusing', Adil later told another Australian journalist. 'We didn't know anything about this invasion. We were very scared and retreated to the second ridge, firing as we went. I was very frightened.'[17] Of the thirty-three young men recruited from his village in 1914, only Adil and two others returned after the war.

By 8 a.m., 8000 Australian and New Zealand troops had been put ashore around Arı Burnu. Only 500 Ottoman troops were in the vicinity to repel them. In some respects, the comparatively light Ottoman resistance was a mixed blessing for the Anzacs. Encouraged by

ANZAC troops coming ashore at Anzac Cove,
around 10.30 a.m., 25 April 1915. *AWM A00834*

their initial success, the invaders rushed inland seeking more men to
kill. But the Allies' grand strategy was not going to plan and the
further the Anzacs pushed inland the more confused things became.
The men had been told they would come ashore facing 200 metres
of open ground which they should run across before tackling the first
hill. Something went wrong—either the navy's navigation was poor
or local currents pushed the small boats off-course. For whatever
reason, the boats beached one-and-a-half kilometres north of the designated landing site. Instead of the open ground, the troops faced steep
cliffs and rugged ravines running virtually down to the water's edge.
Von Sanders had given little thought to defending Arı Burnu because

it was considered too precipitous. Had the men come ashore just north of Gaba Tepe as planned, they would have encountered barbed wire in the water and many more machine guns, hence initial Anzac casualties might have been much heavier. These losses only added to the confusion. Small groups of Australians penetrated deep inland; by 7 a.m., one officer and two scouts actually caught a glimpse of the straits but they, like everyone else, were now completely out of touch with the pre-planned strategy.

First reports of the landing reached Ottoman headquarters at about 5 a.m. and von Sanders was woken. Soon, reports came in of landings up and down the coast, and on the Asiatic side as well. Years later, von Sanders recalled the moment:

> From the many pale faces among the officers reporting in the early morning it became apparent that although a hostile landing had been expected with certainty, a landing at so many places surprised many and filled them with apprehension. My first feeling was that our arrangements needed no change. That was a great satisfaction! The hostile landing expedition had selected those points which we ourselves considered the most likely landing places and had specially prepared for defence.
>
> It seemed improbable to me that extensive landings would take place at all of these places, but we could not discern at that moment where the enemy was actually seeking the decision.[18]

Arı Burnu seemed the only point at which von Sanders's plan was faltering. The Australians had captured the first ridge overlooking the sea and were advancing up Chunuk Bair, a peak 260 metres in height that dominates the entire region. Standing on it, the whole Gallipoli peninsula and the Dardanelles Straits are laid out beneath you. Whoever rules the peak would, in all probability, control the battlefield for kilometres around. It was the Ottomans' good fortune that this fact was instantly grasped by the officer in charge of the area, Lieutenant Colonel Mustafa Kemal. The speed of thought he displayed that morning did much to save a rapidly deteriorating situation. Kemal was born in 1881 at Selanik (today's Thessalonika in northern Greece). His father was a minor government official. Mustafa chose the army as his career and graduated from the War Academy in 1905 with the rank of captain.

Mustafa Kemal peers out from a Gallipoli trench. This image has become part of Turkish folklore. It has been adapted for many uses, such as the 1930s rug reproduced on this book's back cover. *AWM A05319*

In 1918, Kemal recounted his memories of that fateful morning to a journalist:

I was expecting landings around Kaba Tepe and when I heard warships bombing around Arıburnu [Anzac Cove]. It was 6.30 in the morning, a report was received that indicated [the] enemy was climbing up the hills behind Arıburnu. I was requested to provide a battalion to counter the enemy. I suspected that this would be a major landing and my Division would be needed rather than a battalion to match the enemy.

I started the march towards the enemy with the 57th Regiment which was at [the] ready and a mountain battery. This regiment is famous because all of its members were killed. There was no road towards Kocaçimen [Hill 971], and it was such a rough terrain. We finally managed to get to this hill which is the highest on the peninsula. However, Arıburnu was in a blind spot and could not be seen, so I could only observe many boats and warships on the sea. I asked the regiment to have a rest and I walked towards Conkbayırı [Chunuk Bair] with the regimental doctor, the commander of the battery and my lieutenant. As we got there, we saw a group of soldiers running towards us from the Hill 261 [the southern shoulder of Chunuk Bair]. I stopped them and asked them why they were running, they said, 'Sir, the enemy!' and showed a small band of soldiers following them at a distance. Can you imagine, the enemy was closer to me than my troops which I had left behind. I shouted, 'You can not run away from the enemy!'. They said they had no bullets left and I replied, 'If you have no ammunition you have your bayonets' and ordered them to fix bayonets and face the enemy. Upon this action, the enemy soldiers also laid down. In the mean time I asked my lieutenant to urgently bring the regiment's soldiers to this spot.

Pretty soon, the first company arrived. I ordered these soldiers to start firing at the enemy. Also placed the battery into position in a dry creek bed and began firing on the enemy. It was about 10 a.m. Then I received a report that the 27th Regiment also came to the location and began engaging the enemy further below where we were. By 11.30 a.m., the enemy was in retreat.[19]

The crucial role played by Mustafa Kemal during those vital first hours was vividly recalled, at a later date, by Zeki Bey, an Ottoman officer who fought alongside Kemal:

My battalion was on parade when the news of . . . [the] landing came to us . . . It chanced that there had been ordered for that morning an exercise over the ground, especially towards Koja Chemen Tepe [sic] [Hill 971] . . . The commander of our division, the 19th, had received about dawn a report . . . that a landing had occurred at Arı Burnu.

The Turkish staff and commanders concerned did not expect a landing at Arı Burnu . . . because it was too precipitous . . . The message then asked the commander of the 19th Division to send one battalion against Arı Burnu . . .

The Commander of the 19th Division was Mustafa Kemal . . .

The regiment was assembled when the order came. Mustafa Kemal came himself, and ordered to regiment and a battery of artillery—mountain guns—to intercept the 'English' who had landed. He reasoned:

'If this force has gone in the direction of Koja Chemen Tepe [sic], the landing is not a mere demonstration—it is the real thing, the landing is a main force'.

For that reason he took, not one battalion, as the commander of the 9th Division had asked, but the whole regiment. They went at once straight across country towards the south of Koja Chemen Tepe [sic]—towards Chunuk Bair—Kemal himself leading.[20]

The fighting around Arı Burnu ebbed and flowed for the remainder of the day. Gradually, however, the Ottomans reasserted control as they retained almost all of the higher points. This allowed them to look down on to the Anzacs and pick them off as they advanced. By 4 p.m., the Ottomans had driven the invaders off Battleship Hill and nearby Baby 700 and most of Plateau 400. A senior British officer, Major General Sir CE Callwell, later wrote of the day's events:

[It is] difficult to give a connected account of the disjointed encounters that took place during this day of fluctuating battle. The further the assailants pushed inland from the beach the more difficult the terrain became, and the more formidable the resistance of the antagonists, who displayed marked skill in utilising the plentiful cover afforded by the scrub and by the very broken character of the ground.[21]

Von Sanders's defence plan operated even more smoothly down at Cape Helles, the southern tip of the Gallipoli peninsula. A series of small beaches was dotted around the Cape. Behind them a broad plain extended some ten kilometres to Achi Baba, a gently rounded hill 215 metres high commanding the whole foot of the peninsula. Nestled beneath Achi Baba was Krithia, a small village whose inhabitants wisely had fled before the battle began.

The Germans and Ottomans had put considerable thought into the defence of the Cape. Heavy barbed wire was laid in the shallows at most beaches and trenches dug in the best possible defensive positions. As at Gaba Tepe, a single company of 200 men was delegated to defend each beach with the bulk of the Ottoman troops kept back as reserves.

The planned Allied landings at Cape Helles were very different in style to that proposed at Gaba Tepe. Soon after the Australians had gone ashore at Gaba Tepe, British and French battleships would begin bombarding beaches around Cape Helles preparatory to 6000 troops landing at five selected beaches (code named Y, X, W, V, and S—see map p. 50). Another 12 000 troops would disembark once the beach heads were secured.

At 5 a.m. on 25 April, the British battleship *Albion* opened fire on the old Ottoman fort of Sedd-el-Bahr, code-named V beach. Sedd-el-Bahr and nearby W beach were the pivot points for the projected landings. The mighty naval bombardment launched on both beaches forced the local defenders to retreat from the shore and seek whatever protection they could find against the awesome shelling. The barrage kept up for about an hour.

By the time it stopped, the sun was rapidly rising in the sky. The Ottomans ran back to their trenches overlooking the beaches. The tension among the men must have been immense as they crouched and waited. Soon enough, a large collier and a flotilla of small boats became visible heading for shore. The intentions of the six small steamboats, each towing five open boats crammed with British soldiers, seemed clear enough, but why was the large ship steaming straight for the beach at Sedd-el-Bahr? The puzzled men waited and watched, resisting any temptation to open fire too early. The quiet peacefulness continued as the boats approached the shore. The British could have been forgiven for thinking they would walk ashore unopposed.

At 6.22 a.m. the collier, *River Clyde,* grounded in the shallows. At almost the same time, the first of the small boats touched the sand. Immediately, the Ottoman machine gunners sprang into action. A storm of bullets pinged against the *River Clyde*. Others spat into the sand, cutting the British to shreds as they alighted from the open boats. Those few men who were not hit were forced to lie under a low bank and literally were pinned to the beach. Two brave men dived from the *River Clyde* into the sea and managed to lash together some rowboats to make a bridge with the beach. Doors then opened on each side of the ship and troops came running out. Having already beaten off the smaller boats, the Ottoman machine gunners turned all their fire against the *River Clyde*. 'Shrapnel, pompom, machine guns and rifles vied with each other to see which could kill most of these gallant Irishmen.' Hundreds were hit and fell into the water.

The calm sea became 'absolutely red with blood'.[22] Mercifully, the British called a halt to the carnage.

The thousand or so men still inside the *River Clyde* waited through the long day then alighted after dark without molestation. Once ashore they attempted to take the Sedd-el-Bahr fort but the alert Ottomans easily beat them off.

Things went equally disastrously for the Allies at nearby W beach. Only about ninety Ottomans survived the heavy naval bombardment but they occupied stout trenches with perfect lines of fire across the beach. As at V beach, the Ottomans held back their fire until the boats virtually hit shore. One English major noted as he was rowed towards the shore that the place seemed deserted. 'About 200 yards [183 metres] from the beach', wrote another English soldier, 'the tows were cast off and the boats shot ahead in line, and the sailors rowed like mad. At about 100 yards [ninety-one metres] from the beach the enemy opened fire, and bullets came thick all round, splashing up the water.'[23] An English captain describes what happened next:

> There was tremendously strong barbed wire where my boat landed. Men were being hit in the boats and as they splashed ashore. I got to my waist in water, tripped over a rock and went under, got up and made for the shore and lay down by the barbed wire. There was a man there before me shouting for wire-cutters. I got mine out, but could not make the slightest impression. The front of the wire was by now a thick mass of men, the majority of whom never moved again. The trenches on the right raked us and those above us raked our right, while trenches and machine guns fired straight down the valley. The noise was ghastly and the sights horrible . . .[24]

Some Ottomans even stood up above their trench to get a clearer shot. 'The sea behind me was absolutely crimson and you could hear the groans through the rattle of musketry', one invader remembers.[25] The barbed wire petered out near the north end of the beach, thus allowing some British to get ashore comparatively safely, clamber up the cliff and return the Ottoman fire. One English soldier later recalled:

> The weight of our packs tired us, so that we could only gasp for breath. After a little time we fixed bayonets and started up the cliffs right and left.

On the right several were blown by a mine. When we started up the cliff
the enemy went, but when we got to the top they were ready and poured
shots on us. After a breather in the enemy trenches above, we pushed on
. . . and had an awful time. The place was strewn. I could see them being
shot all around as we lay before advancing again.[26]

The small Ottoman force was compelled to give ground. By mid-
morning, British troops from W beach had linked up with the men
landed at the adjoining beach X and threatened to capture the high
ground above Cape Helles. However, this was not to be, for as one
historian of the campaign writes: 'The Turks had not only carefully
prepared this position but had occupied the emplacement of Fort
Helles which gave excellent cover for infantry and was just far
enough to the eastward to command the high ground, so in spite of
determined efforts and artillery preparation by the fleet which took
a hand in the affair after 1 p.m., the Turks remained in possession
and in fact during the afternoon and night delivered counter attacks
on the invaders which forced the British to employ every rifle in the
fighting line.'[27]

The landings at the three other beaches were made good with
very few casualties. In fact, only four Turks were found in the neigh-
bourhood of Y beach, a rugged isolated spot which the defenders had
considered an unlikely landing point. Two thousand men went
ashore there. They climbed the cliff then sat down and brewed a cup
of tea while their officers discussed what to do next. Two of the
officers actually walked into the deserted Krithia village. While the
British procrastinated, the Ottomans were rushing reinforcements
into the area. By mid-afternoon, Y beach was under attack and the
British tommies began digging trenches. The chance to advance had
been lost—no Allied soldier ever again set foot in Krithia during the
entire campaign.

In addition to the Gaba Tepe and Cape Helles landings,
Hamilton organised two dummy landings. British ships massed in
Saros Bay (the extreme north of the peninsula) as if about to disem-
bark a large landing force. Meanwhile, across the straits, 3000 French
troops were put ashore at Kum Kale. Both schemes worried the
Ottoman High Command but neither proved a decisive handicap.
Ironically, the French at Kum Kale were the only attackers to achieve

The shattered main street of Krithia, photographed in 1919. *AWM G02057*

The same street in 2002. Krithia has been renamed Alçıtepe. *H. H. Başarın*

all the tasks set for them. They seized a ruined fort and captured 500 Ottoman troops at a cost of 600 French casualties. No sooner had they gained this success than they were instructed to re-embark and assist the beleagured British at Cape Helles. In strategic terms, the success counted for little as von Sanders was already ferrying regiments from Çanakkale to Maidos. He now appreciated that an invasion on the Asiatic coast was far less threatening to the straits and İstanbul than the possible loss of the Gallipoli peninsula.

The overall battle picture remained confused for both sides throughout the day. The Allies could take heart from the many localised victories they had won, and from the fact that they had secured footholds at both Arı Burnu and Cape Helles. Equally, however, the Ottoman defence had been most meritorious. Their forces were heavily outnumbered throughout the day on both major fronts yet nowhere had their line been seriously breached. At Cape Helles, for example, two Ottoman battalions had repulsed twelve Allied battalions put ashore at five different beaches. The Allies had found in the Ottoman a courageous, skilled fighter who made full use of the terrain. Many Allied soldiers could not even catch sight of the enemy, let alone kill them. A New Zealand private who landed late on 25 April wrote in his diary two days later: 'not fired a shot yet, neither have any of the rest of my platoon'.[28] A British soldier made a similar observation a few days later:

> At eleven o'clock we moved up . . . in Indian file until we were in open country and then spread out, advancing in short rushes. Immediately in front of us was a swamp which we were ordered to cross. The Turkish fire was murderous and we lost a lot of men. There were no trenches to be seen but the Turks must have had their machine-guns perfectly sighted. It was terrifying; fewer men rose after each rush but we still charged forward blindly, repeatedly changing directions, but it did not appear to make the slightest difference. The fire was coming from all directions yet we could not see a single Turk or any sign of a trench . . . We took stock of our position; we had not yet fired a single round. If we could only get a glimpse of a single Turk we would have some idea of the direction we should take . . .[29]

It would be wrong, however, to think that the defenders had things all their own way. Many Ottoman positions were overrun by sheer weight of numbers and neither side felt any obligation to take prisoners. One great advantage the Allies enjoyed was the availability of heavy naval artillery to support their land forces. Liman von Sanders commented that the Allied naval guns 'completely covered the southern part of the peninsula with their fire from three sides . . . The enemy ships protected the landed troops in the fullest sense of the word. We on our side in those days had nothing but field artillery . . . [T]he Dardanelles Campaign is the only great operation in the World War where a land army had to do steady battle against a hostile army and navy . . .'[30] The naval gunners constantly strove to unsettle the Ottomans and ease the strain on their own army. 'Just before dark [on 25 April] the three ships off V Beach opened a savage bombardment on Turkish defences', comments the English Rear-Admiral, RJB Keyes. 'The enemy's position was obliterated in sheets of flame and clouds of yellow smoke and dust from our [British] high explosive, and under its cover we could see men rise from behind the sandbank and take shelter under the seaward face of the fort. It seemed incredible that anyone could be left alive in the enemy's position, but when the fire was lifted that ghastly tat-tat-tat of machine-gun fire broke out again, and took toll of anyone who moved.'[31] A British midshipman witnessed a similar scene: 'We opened fire on the Turks with twelve-pounders . . . I could see a dozen of them rush out of their trench, run fifty yards [forty-six metres], lie flat with our men's rifle bullet splashes all around them. When we directed our fire at them I saw a lot of heads, legs and arms go up in the air; however, they fought very bravely and made a very good effort to rush the French trenches, and no doubt would have succeeded had it not been for us.'[32]

By nightfall on 25 April, both armies had fought themselves virtually to a standstill. The casualty figures were horrific. Two Ottoman regiments, to take but one example, had lost 2000 men or nearly half their total strength. There were instances on both sides of small units practically being wiped out. Those men who had got through unscathed were by now exhausted and, more often than not, totally disorganised in terms of supplies and leadership.

Ironically, neither set of commanders appreciated the plight of their opponent; they were too busy trying to bolster morale among their own men and planning how to survive the approaching day. The information reaching Mustafa Kemal during the night was so muddled that towards morning he toured the front to see for himself how many troops he still possessed and what condition they were in. Things were viewed even more seriously within the Allies' lines. Senior Australian officers were so distressed by the day's events and the plight of their men that late in the evening they sought permission to evacuate their entire force. Hamilton rejected the request on the grounds that there was insufficient time remaining before daybreak to effect an evacuation. The Australians were convinced that once daylight returned, the Ottomans would launch a massive counterattack and try to drive the invaders back into the sea. They were thus most surprised and heartened when the sun rose but no Ottoman attack eventuated.

Sporadic, localised fighting, sometimes quite fierce, occurred throughout the day but neither side organised a major attack. Instead, both attacker and defender used the day to reassess the position and bring in troop reinforcements. One Ottoman regiment at Arı Burnu consisted entirely of Arabs who some senior officers thought might not be reliable in battle. So, during the afternoon of 26 April, other units were brought up to support them. Down at Cape Helles, the British evacuated Y beach. They left behind large quantities of equipment and ammunition which the Ottomans quickly seized. The general level of fear and uncertainty can be judged from a message sent during the day by an Ottoman officer at Cape Helles:

My Captain—the enemy's infantry is taking cover at the back of the Sedd-el-Bahr gun defences, but the rear of these gun defences cannot come under fire . . . With the twenty or twenty-five men I have with me it will not be possible to drive them off with a bayonet charge, because I am obliged to spread my men out. Either you must send up reinforcements and drive the enemy into the sea, or let us evacuate this place, because I am absolutely certain that they will land more men tonight . . .

Send the doctors to carry off my wounded. Alas! Alas! My Captain, for God's sake send me reinforcements, because hundreds of soldiers are landing. Hurry up. What on earth will happen, my Captain? From Abdul Rahman.[33]

The commanders of both armies regarded Cape Helles as the key sector. Accordingly, most of their attention was focused there. The Anzac Cove area was considered less dangerous as any rapid advance was virtually impossible in such rugged terrain. Hence, most of the fresh units which arrived on 26 April were sent to Cape Helles, and Mustafa Kemal was asked to drive the infidel into the sea with few reinforcements. He ordered his men to keep their distance from the still numerically superior enemy force 'so as to guard against its bayonet assault, and thus [avoid] defeat'. His plan succeeded and the brittle line held. What he did not know, of course, was that the generals opposing him feared their own defeat was imminent, just as he did. It was a day when both armies regarded survival as a victory. Kemal has written of it: 'The 26 April was a victory and not a defeat. This was not an example of our soldier's [sic] greatest self-sacrifice or heroism because I remember days on which Turks showed greater self-sacrifice than this. Anyway, it was an important day won thanks to the firmness and tenacity of our troops and the bravery and determination of our officers and commanders.'[34]

Kemal renewed his attack when two fresh regiments joined his forces late on 26 April. Next day, his forces made several charges. They consolidated their hold on the important points Baby 700, Battleship Hill and Plateau 400, but only with heavy losses. Nowhere did they break through the Allied line entirely. At 9 p.m., for example, 'wild blowing of bugles and all manner of shouting' warned the Anzacs that the Ottomans were surging towards them. The Official Australian War Historian records that 'they came on with great bravery, even crawling to the Australian trench and firing into it'.[35] The attack was repulsed within the hour but others followed during the night.

While the Anzacs clung to their tenuous position, down at Cape Helles the British and French were planning how best to push on with their attack. An unsuccessful assault was made on Krithia village during the morning of 28 April. By now, bitter experience had demonstrated to both sides (if they cared to learn the lesson) that frontal assaults against enemy trenches were almost certainly doomed to fail even when attackers greatly outnumbered defenders unless something (darkness, covering artillery fire, gas, or the like) could somehow lessen the wall of bullets that otherwise met each and every attack. The gruesome reality of such attacks was summed up in one Australian's diary: 'these . . . Turks . . . were simply mowed down like hay before the mower'.[36]

By the time darkness fell on 28 April, the battle had stabilised around Arı Burnu and Cape Helles. The Allies' second great attempt to open the Narrows had failed, just as did the first. The Allied troops were exhausted and few fresh units were available to replace or assist them. The Ottomans had managed to bring up enough reinforcements to arrest the invasion.

FOUR

# '. . . a brave and tenacious enemy'

It is sometimes said that ignorance is bliss. When you do not know any better, you can hold all the prejudices and misconceptions you like. Once you know someone or something, so often it is hard to go on accepting your old ideas, for now you can judge things on the basis of your own experience rather than rely on hearsay or prejudice. Such was the case on Gallipoli. As the weeks went by after the landings, the men from all nations learned that the pre-battle propaganda they had received about the 'beastly' enemy was largely wrong. This chapter explores these changes in perception.

In chapter three we learned that few men on either side had any clear idea about the troops they would be fighting. For most men, the stereotypical enemy soldier was Godless, cruel and bloodthirsty. Virtually every country at war attempts to construct such a picture of its opponent in order to make people hate the enemy so much they are willing to sacrifice their lives or the lives of their loved ones rather than submit to, or make peace with, the dreaded foe. The Gallipoli campaign was no different to other wars: the men of both armies strode into battle, their heads filled with a strong sense of self-preservation and a deep hatred for the enemy. As one Australian put it in his diary: '[We sailed] . . . off to death and "Glory". What fools we are, men mad. The Turk he comes at one, with the blood lust in his eyes, shouts Allah! Australian like, we swear "Kill or be killed . . ."'[1] Just how mistaken one could be about the enemy is shown by the cry of an Australian as he fired on the first day: 'Take that you black b.....s.'[2]

It took some time for these preconceptions to fade. All sorts of rumours circulated among the men during those confused first days. On 27 April a wounded Australian reported: 'We have one man here with his tongue cut out, another lay wounded and a Turk cried "Australian" and drove his bayonet in, but was shot and the bayonet's work was not completed.'[3] There were other rumours of Ottoman and German troops masquerading in British uniforms, or that they were using 'dum dum' bullets banned by international law because of the ghastly wounds they caused.

As the days passed, the Allied troops rapidly became aware of the real (as distinct from imagined) mettle of the Ottomans and the reality of war. War was hell; the enemy soldiers were much like themselves. Only a week after the landings, a British staff officer told his wife in a letter: '[The Turks] are treating our wounded splendidly! So believe no other stories you may hear.'[4] All evidence suggested that the Ottoman was as courageous as he was humane. A British soldier wrote of one unsuccessful Turkish attack early in May: 'It was incredible that men could still come forward but they did, and some came so near that they fell into our ditch, their fighting days over. They just added to the many that already lay around but their courage will live long in my mind.'[5] Everyone was reassessing his opinion. 'The Turkish positions only get stronger every day. We gave them such a lot of warning. They are magnificently led, well-armed, and very brave and numerous', a British chaplain commented on 18 May.[6] A week earlier, a prominent English war correspondent attached to the British Army reported to his readers: 'We face a brave and tenacious enemy.'[7]

Undoubtedly, this change of heart was induced partly by the need to explain why the Allies had not been able to defeat the Ottomans as quickly or as easily as had been expected. A journalist could hardly write that the enemy was ill-trained and undermanned then admit they were nevertheless providing more than a match for the British Army! Clearly, some self-interest was involved. It still seems, however, that the revision of attitudes was largely genuine. Anyone who watched the Ottomans in action had to admit they were a determined, resourceful fighting force. An Ottoman general proudly reported in a letter to his father: 'The Germans are astonished at the bravery and self-sacrifice of our soldiers . . .'[8]

Weeks passed with no sign of the stalemate ending. The Allies could regard this as some sort of victory; they had established a foothold on Ottoman soil and the Ottomans seemingly could not dislodge them. National pride as much as any military necessity would demand that the Ottoman Army make every effort not merely to restrain the Allies but drive them off the peninsula. The nineteenth of May was set as the date for this great attack. The Anzac zone was chosen over Cape Helles because, as one Ottoman officer later explained:

> The position at Anzac was without parallel in history. The opposing trenches were so close together and the Anzac Corps line was very close to the sea; consequently they were much confined and would make every effort to enlarge their positions. It was therefore better for the Turks to have the initiative and attack before the Anzac troops attacked . . . If this attack succeeded, a force of some four or five Turkish divisions would be freed, and available to deal with Sedd-el-Bahr [Cape Helles] . . . The proximity of the trenches was an advantage in making a surprise attack.[9]

A British reconnaissance aircraft spotted a fresh division of Ottoman troops landing at Maidos on 18 May. Other units were also observed marching towards the Anzac area from Krithia, hence the Allies had ample warning of the impending attack. The Ottoman plan was for 42 000 men to attack before daybreak, drive the Anzacs from their trenches and pursue them down to the sea. Included in the force were a number of young officer-cadets sent from training school in İstanbul.

The *Official Australian History* conveys a sense of the tense atmosphere that developed as the night progressed:

> So, during the night of 18 May, while the Turkish troops were being silently crowded into and in rear of their front trenches in preparation for their secret attack before dawn, on the other side of the same crests the rifles had been carefully cleaned and oiled, and officers and orderlies were now hurrying among the sleeping supports to ensure that everything should be in readiness to meet the expected assault. At 11.35 the moon went down. Ten minutes later, following upon the explosion of a bomb at Quinn's Post, the Turkish rifle fire suddenly increased until its roar surpassed that of any fusillade which the Australian troops experienced in

the war. Along the whole Anzac line the assumption for the moment was that this must be the prelude to the attack.[10]

The fire slackened within half an hour. The Turks hoped this barrage might be mistaken by the Australians as the real attack and thus entice them to lower their vigilance once it ended. The ploy failed; just before 3 a.m. the Anzac troops were awakened and told to keep sharp lookout.

Hardly any time had passed before figures were seen in the dim light emerging from the Ottoman trenches. 'The sky was, for that hour, exceptionally clear, and the pale light could be seen reflected from sheaves of long, thin Turkish bayonets.'[11] At first the Ottomans crept forward in silence but as they got nearer the Anzac trenches they shouted 'Allah! Allah!' and charged ahead. An Australian describes what it was like to face such an attack:

> We were wide awake now, surely an attack was meditated. Yes! The enemy was advancing in mass formation. Our fellows had received orders to allow the Turks to come within ten paces and then to pour the lead into them. Our rifles held eleven cartridges, and are, in every way, very formidable little weapons.
> 'Allah! Allah! Allah!'
> They are coming with leaps and bounds, their dismal, howling cry rending the night. Closer and closer, they are almost upon us! 'Fire!' yells an officer.
> We comply willingly, rifles crack and rattle all down our line, the high-pitched music of machine guns being audible above the din.[12]

What a withering hail of lead met those dusky warriors.

The men were stirred on by martial music played by an Ottoman military band hidden very near the front line. The densely packed lines of men surged forward only to be cut down by the Anzacs' rifles. 'Many Australians mounted the parapet, and sitting astride upon it, fired continuously, as in an enormous drive of game', Australia's official historian later wrote.[13] At places, the Ottomans succeeded in entering enemy trenches but each incursion was repulsed with bayonet and bullet. The Ottoman general allowed the senseless slaughter to continue for nearly eight hours before calling a halt. Once the terrific din subsided, the pitiful cries of badly wounded men lying untended in no-man's land could be heard only too clearly. That afternoon, the Australians counted three thousand dead in front of their own trenches. Whole companies had been wiped out. The Anzacs, by comparison, had only 160 men killed and 468 wounded. Australian rifles and machine guns fired 948 000 bullets repulsing these suicidal attacks. Rifle barrels became too hot to touch as men shot until they 'were almost tired of slaughter'.[14]

Everywhere one looked between the lines, dead and wounded lay in their hundreds. No-one who witnessed the sight could ever forget it. CEW Bean, the Australian war correspondent and historian of Gallipoli states:

> The names given by the [Ottomans] . . . to the Anzac hills almost certainly tell the story of this fight. Lone Pine became Kanli Sirt, 'Bloody Ridge'; Johnston's Jolly—Kirmezi Sirt, 'Red Ridge' [sic]; No-Man's Land near the Pimple—Shehidlar Tepe, 'Martyrs' Hill'; Plugge's Plateau—Khain Tepe, 'Treacherous Hill' [sic].[15]

The dead lie stiff and bloated in no-man's land after the Ottoman attack of 19 May. *AWM H03955*

Any doubts the Anzacs might have held about the bravery of the Ottoman soldier disappeared that morning. So, too, went all those ideas that the Turks used 'dum dum' bullets and the like, for the Anzacs now saw only too graphically the horrific injuries their own bullets could inflict. Bean noticed one body with 'half the head blown away'. He saw another head wound 'like a star, or pane of broken glass; another more or less circular—you could put your hand into either'.[16]

Ottoman respect for the Anzacs also rose considerably. A senior Ottoman officer told Bean after the war: 'In this attack the worth of the Anzac soldiers in defence was realised; they shot well and used their machine-guns to the best advantage.'[17] This, however, did not mean the Ottomans were any less determined to continue the fight. In the afternoon, Australians at Quinn's Post (where the opposing trenches were less than ten metres apart) threw over a note urging their foe to surrender. The reply tossed back read: 'You think there are no true Turks left. But there are Turks, and Turks' sons!'[18]

The scene grew ever more pitiful as the day went on. 'Everywhere you looked the dead men lay, and hours later you might see an arm or a leg rise, where some poor fellow cried on death not to delay. In time the breath of decay searched you out the length of Shrapnel Valley, and when the wind veered in the trenches it caught you by the throat. I marvelled how the men there got down their dinners.'[19] The next day turned into the hottest of the campaign thus far. Flies swarmed in their millions over the rotting corpses. The bodies swelled up to incredible sizes in the hot sun, the skin turning black. It was clear that something had to be done to bury the dead before the rotting flesh encouraged still more flies and disease. But how could any burials take place when even the slightest movement above the trench instantly attracted the attention of enemy snipers?

During the afternoon some Australians hoisted a Red Cross flag above their parapet. Two bullets pierced it immediately. Then an Ottoman messenger jumped up, ran forward and apologised, saying many Ottoman soldiers did not know the significance of the flag. An impromptu ceasefire was thereupon arranged in the area and stretcher bearers from both sides began carrying off the dead. While this was happening, an Australian general stood in no-man's land chatting in French with several Ottoman officers and exchanging cigarettes with them. As they spoke, he noticed an Ottoman soldier collecting rifles from some corpses. Feeling that this breached the spirit of the ceasefire, the Australian ordered his men back into their trench. He told the Ottomans any further ceasefire must be arranged formally between the commanding officers.

Two days later, the Ottomans sent out a colonel to negotiate terms for a temporary armistice. Armed with a white flag, he was escorted to Anzac Headquarters where it was agreed to stop fighting between 7.30 a.m. and 4.30 p.m. on 24 May so that both sides might bury their dead. Groups from each army would collect bodies in their half of no-man's land, bury their own dead and return the corpses of enemy soldiers for burial.

After a month of continual fighting and ceaseless noise, the sudden tranquillity seemed unreal. 'The silence was very strange', wrote one Australian.[20] It was a welcome chance to stretch without fear of being shot. For the first time in many weeks, men could stand and survey the whole landscape. It was also a unique opportunity to

Anzac troops stand back and stare as the blindfolded Ottoman staff officer prepares to remount his horse late in the afternoon on 22 May after negotiating terms for an armistice. *AWM J02401*

meet the enemy. Men stepped up to the ceasefire line and swapped smiles, photographs, cigarettes and small gifts with each other. An Australian ambulance officer found the Ottomans 'peaceful-looking men, stolid in type and of the peasant class mostly. We fraternised with them and gave them cigarettes and tobacco. Some Germans were there, but they viewed us with malignant eyes. When I talked to Colonel Pope about it afterwards he said the Germans were a mean lot of beggars: "Why" said he most indignantly, "they came and had a look into my trenches." I asked "What did you do?" He replied, "Well, I had a look at theirs."'[21]

The digging was arduous work, so both sides chose their biggest men for the burial parties. Shallow graves were excavated and the dead were buried where they lay. Mercifully, the day was cool, but it was a vile task nonetheless. '[T]he stench is sickening. The burial party has indeed a horrible job,' noted one Australian.[22] A Salvation Army padre wrote to his wife that it had been 'the most dreadful experience even I have had . . . I retched and have been sleepless since . . . No words can describe the ghastliness'.[23] Another Australian felt eternally grateful to the Ottoman medico who gave him pieces of scented wool to block his nostrils. Before the day was through, some four thousand bodies had been buried. At 4.30 p.m., as arranged, the men climbed back down into their trenches. 'Both sides parted as friends', one soldier noted.[24] An Australian remembers swapping his bully beef and biscuits for Turkish dates and figs. Folklore has it that an Anzac called out to an Ottoman, 'Good-bye, old chap; good luck!' Back came the reply in Turkish, 'Smiling may you go and smiling come again!'[25] At 4.45 p.m., a single shot rang out. Soon, the chatter of rifle fire returned to its normal level. That night, an Australian wrote in his diary: 'The time was taken up by making friends with the Turks, who do not seem to be a very bad sort of chap after all.'[26]

The 19 May debacle only confirmed yet again the futility of sending lines of men 'over the top' against machine guns. Other means had to be found if the deadlock was to be resolved. The Ottomans had already begun exploring such alternatives. On 9 May they began digging tunnels from their own front line towards the Allied trenches at Quinn's Post. Quinn's was a vital point in

Burying the dead during the armistice, 24 May. Soldiers from both sides moved about freely during the day, working alongside each other digging communal graves. In taking this photograph, Lieutenant-Colonel Charles Ryan of the Australian Army Medical Corps was contravening the terms of the armistice. *AWM H03954*

the Anzac line for it commanded a view right down Monash and Shrapnel gullies to the sea. If the Ottomans could capture the post, it would become very difficult for the Anzacs to send reinforcements and supplies up to the front line. As the tunnelling edged towards their trenches, the Australians began to hear the 'tap, tap' noise of pick and shovel at work. They started tunnels of their own. By 25 May, these Australian listening posts were sure the Ottomans were only a few feet away. Small explosive charges were brought up and the listening posts blown up. Part of a Turkish tunnel was destroyed and its tunnellers buried alive.

Despite this setback, the Ottomans resumed digging immediately. Two days later, the Allies again tried unsuccessfully to stop them. At 3.20 a.m. on 29 May, 'a series of loud and heavy explosions . . . shook the valley'.[27] The Turks had exploded a mine a few metres in front of Quinn's Post. As earth and debris showered down on the Australians, Ottoman troops rushed forward throwing small hand bombs. They quickly seized some thirty metres of Australian trench. The defenders rallied, however, before Ottoman reinforcements could be sent over to make good the gains. Part of the trench was quickly recaptured but the remaining Ottomans held out for several hours before accepting the inevitable and surrendering.

Although the attack failed, success had been so near as to suggest that tunnelling might become a most useful tactic. Consequently, digging started in earnest on both sides. It was not a job for the faint-hearted as, more often that not, the miners could hear the enemy burrowing towards them. Hearing their 'tap, tap, tapping' stop was an even more ominous warning, for it suggested that the enemy tunnel was perhaps finished and being loaded with explosives prior to detonation. Many miners were buried alive in these blasts. As the campaign went on, mining techniques became more and more sophisticated and the mines deeper and longer. Special mining units were formed, manned by skilled men such as coal miners. The Anzacs always dug their tunnels with flat ceilings, whereas the Ottomans excavated curved, circular ceilings. Mines were a constant worry for any frontline soldier. 'It was as if one was sitting on a volcano . . .', wrote a German historian. 'Whole areas were turned into a crater desert.'[28]

Another way of breaking the deadlock was to sever the armies' lifeline—the sea. The Allies relied wholly on naval transport to supply its army and provide heavy artillery support. The degree of dependence was not so absolute for the Ottomans as their supplies could be brought in by land, but passage down the Sea of Marmara was much quicker than via the rather primitive roads. When the land fighting ground to a halt, naval warfare again appeared an attractive option despite its earlier disasters. A telling blow was struck in the misty early hours of 12 May when the Turkish torpedo boat *Muavanet-i-Milliye* slipped unnoticed through the straits and torpedoed the British battleship *Goliath*. Six hundred and eighteen officers and men were drowned. Yet, despite this success, German and Ottoman admirals knew they did not have sufficient ships seriously to challenge the Allied fleet. Neither the *Yavuz* nor the *Midilli* (the two German ships attached to the Ottoman Navy) ever left İstanbul during the eight and a half months of the Gallipoli campaign. But if the Allies could not be beaten on the seas, they were not necessarily invincible beneath the waves.

As chance would have it, a German submarine, U-boat *21*, had set out for İstanbul on 25 April. The long voyage around Britain and through the Mediterranean took it nearly a month. The scene that greeted its crew off Gallipoli was a submariner's dream. Large numbers of battleships and support vessels were moored peacefully like sitting ducks. Submarine nets were strung around the larger ships to 'catch' torpedoes but no-one put much faith in their ability. At noon on 25 May, *U21* fired a torpedo at the Royal Navy battleship *Triumph* off Gaba Tepe. Within fifteen minutes the massive ship had turned bottom-up although almost the entire crew was saved. Fighting in the trenches virtually came to a stop as everyone watched this symbol of British naval might disappear before them. The Ottomans held back their fire while survivors were rescued from the sea. The commanding British admiral immediately ordered the fleet to retire to the safety of the Greek island of Imbros, nineteen kilometres from the mainland. Two days later, *Majestic*, the one battleship still stationed near the coast, was sunk by torpedo off Cape Helles. The sinkings were a marvellous tonic for Ottoman morale after the devastating losses of 19 May. For the second time in as many months, the Allied fleet had turned tail and run.

The Ottomans' rejoicing was short-lived indeed, for, only an hour after the *Triumph* was hit, a British submarine torpedoed and sank the storeship *Stamboul* moored off İstanbul. Panic swept through the city with people believing the long-expected invasion was commencing. Two weeks earlier, another British submarine had sunk an Ottoman troopship in the Sea of Marmara, drowning almost all aboard. The sinkings forced the Ottomans to send their re-inforcements overland rather than by sea as before. The journey from İstanbul was thus transformed from a short overnight voyage to a rail trip over 240 kilometres and a five-day trudge along very bad roads. The British submarines harassed Ottoman shipping throughout the year. Liman von Sanders claimed after the war that had the British managed to increase their undersea offensive the fifth Army would have been starved. Luckily for him, Britain's war leaders refused to acknowledge the submarines' potential so the strategy was never really encouraged.

The life of a submariner was extremely dangerous as the craft were quite frail and mechanically most unreliable. The crew of the Australian submarine, the *AE2*, were forced to surrender on 30 April when a fault in the main ballast tank forced it to surface in the Narrows only a hundred metres from the Ottoman torpedo boat, *Sultanhisar*. The *AE2* had slipped through the Dardanelles early on 25 April and spent the next few days playing a deadly game of hide-and-seek with local gunboats. When the submarine was finally disabled, her crew was rescued by the torpedo boat and taken to the small town of Gallipoli where Liman von Sanders and his staff inspected them. The men's clothing were soaking wet so the Ottomans kitted them out with a clean, dry, if somewhat ludicrous assortment of Ottoman uniforms. That evening, the Australians were transported by torpedo boat to İstanbul along with a French soldier and an English soldier taken prisoner at the landing.

Word of the *AE2* capture had spread quickly and a large crowd was waiting when the boat docked. 'The crowd kept very quiet showing no hostility towards us', wrote one *AE2* crewman, Herbert Brown, in his diary. 'The only thing one could notice was a few smiling faces. No wonder for I expect we were enough to make anybody laugh [wearing such odd clothes].' The prisoners were marched through the streets to jail, passing along the way the great central railway station decorated with German, Austrian and Ottoman flags. 'Very little notice was taken of us by the populace', Brown noted. 'A few people running to each street corner to see us pass, nothing was shouted at us, a few children were following but if they came too near the Sentries would bang them and they would give up the chase . . . This city which had looked so beautiful from the harbour was soon seen to be otherwise. The streets were narrow and very badly paved and the shops were very poor.'[29]

The Ottoman torpedo boat *Sultanhisar*, which crippled the Australian submarine *AE2* by shelling its engine room after the submarine had inadvertently surfaced nearby. In July 1998 *AE2* was found 73 metres beneath the surface of the Sea of Marmara by a Turkish team led by Selçuk Kolay, Director of the Rahmi M. Koç Museum, İstanbul. *Kindly lent by S. Kolay and Dr. M. Spencer*

At the jail they were greeted by a small group of British, Australian and French troops captured at the landings and shipped to İstanbul the previous day. Another dozen or so men arrived over the next few days. On 5 May everyone was ferried across the Bosphorus, then put on a train destined for the prisoner of war camp at Afyonkarahisar, a small town in Anatolia. The camp housed Russian as well as Gallipoli prisoners, but its numbers were never large as neither side took many prisoners on Gallipoli. The fact that only seventy Australians were captured during the entire campaign gives some indication of the ferocity with which the battles were fought.

Initially, conditions in the camp were not good. 'Our treatment by the Turks . . . was terrible, they made no allowances for cleanliness, we starved', claimed one Australian.[30] Things improved, however, in mid-July after a government official came from İstanbul and met with a deputation of prisoners. The men now received meat twice a day and the camp canteen improved its stock and dropped its prices. Beds were supplied where previously the men had slept on the hard floor. 'All this made our life much happier', noted another prisoner, John Wheat, a naval rating from the *AE2*.[31]

The American Ambassador visited the camp early in August and arranged for regular supplies of fresh food and money to be sent each month.

> After this, instead of living on practically dry bread, we commenced living on bacon and eggs, sausages etc. We very soon began to feel the benefit of this good living. On the fifteenth of August we were visited by another Turkish Officer from Headquarters. He asked for complaints and expressed his pleasure when we told him that things had improved vastly. He also said that he wished us to be happy.[32]

During the day the prisoners were put to work on road-making gangs. In July they helped bring in the harvest. Wheat comments that 'one thing we were surprised at was whenever we were going or returning from work the populace never showed any signs of hate against us, only the children who made signs of cutting our throats, we did not take any notice of that as they were only children.'[33] Quite often, large groups of soldiers camped overnight near the POW camp on their way to the Dardanelles. Often, the troops walked over to peer, for the first time, at the 'infidels' who had invaded their country.

In September, a leading Ottoman newspaper reproduced a letter reputedly first published in the English press:

> The British soldiers who are taken prisoner by the Turks do not complain at all even though the European countries treat POWs very badly and deprive them of food and other things. A journalist from our newspaper has given us a letter from his cousin who is a POW in a small Anatolian town. The letter reads: 'We live in one of the best houses in the town. Turkish soldiers treat us with respect and kindness. I receive the equivalent of the salary of a Turkish officer of the same rank, which is more than enough. I live with three Australians, eight British and six submarine officers. There are also two French and twelve Russians. We have been busy gardening. But then grasshoppers attacked and ate everything but our tomatoes. We had such nice melons, cucumbers and broadbeans.'[34]

A new commandant arrived that month who tightened up the conditions.

Back on Gallipoli, the fighting had disintegrated after 19 May into mainly localised skirmishes. It became a matter of personal pride to establish ascendancy over the enemy in your sector. Trenches were constantly improved, defences strengthened and sniping skills honed. At Lone Pine, the Ottomans laid pine log roofing over their trenches, while at nearby Johnston's Jolly, trench walls were bricked and concrete steps constructed.

The Ottomans enjoyed the better natural position along most of the line, particularly in the Anafartalar (Anzac) sector. Much of the terrain behind their lines sloped away relatively gently, thereby enabling them to locate their guns virtually wherever they wished and move them if they were spotted. The steep slopes on the Anzac side, by comparison, made it very difficult to site, let alone relocate,

This loop-hole plate was positioned in the front line by an Australian marksman for a few days in July to improve his protection. The accuracy of the Ottoman snipers can be judged by the many bullet marks it bears. *AWM 01002*

artillery. Once the fleet retired, artillery support was minimal. The loss was psychological more than material, as the low-trajectory naval guns were not suited to trench warfare and inflicted relatively little damage. A British soldier at Cape Helles who earlier had derived great comfort from watching the navy bombard the enemy lines was bitterly disappointed when, on 4 June, he finally saw inside an Ottoman trench. 'With a mad rush we reached the Turkish trench and jumped in. It must have been ten feet deep and was practically untouched. Where had all our shells gone?'[35] Above-ground structures did not fare so well; there was not a single complete house anywhere on the peninsula by July.

Most trenches ran roughly north–south, so the sun rose behind the Ottoman lines and set behind the Allies. Whether either army gained any advantage from this is debatable. The Ottomans felt at an advantage in the late afternoon when very clear silhouettes of Allied

These Ottoman huts near Lone Pine were considerably safer and more comfortable than any shelters on the Anzac side of the line. They had a thick roof of pine logs covered with earth, topped by corrugated iron and another layer of earth. Most of the huts had fireplaces and brick or board floors. *AWM G01796*

soldiers appeared against the evening sky. Conversely, Allied snipers also enjoyed these hours because the Ottoman had the sun in his eyes.

The hot summer sun beat down relentlessly on everyone. The Allies had the sea in which to bathe and cool off but they were desperately short of drinking water. The Ottomans, by comparison, had many freshwater wells close by but no swimming holes. One problem common to all was the flies; as the weather warmed up, their numbers reached plague proportions. 'The inside tent walls were black with them', recalls a German officer. 'Despite eating with care one would always get some flies into the mouth with every bite. We only tolerated this plague more willingly, when we gathered from English newspapers, that our enemies on the other side suffered even more from them.'[36] An Australian's recollections are even more vivid:

> Immediately I opened . . . [my tin of jam] the flies rushed [it] . . . all fighting amongst themselves. I wrapped my overcoat over the tin and gouged out the flies, then spread the biscuit, held my hand over it, and drew the biscuit out of the coat. But a lot of flies flew into my mouth and beat about the inside . . . I nearly howled with rage . . . Of all the bastards of places this is the greatest bastard in the world.[37]

The heat and flies produced an epidemic of dysentery among the Allied troops. The Ottomans suffered much less from such illnesses, possibly due to their more reliable water supply.

Some relief from the heat was obtainable via the fresh coastal winds which blow in the region. These breezes were probably also the reason why poisonous gas was never used on Gallipoli. This ghastly new weapon was introduced to the Western Front by both Germany and Britain early in 1915 and respirators were issued to British units on Gallipoli. The peninsula winds would have dispersed the gas quite quickly and thereby greatly reduced its potency.

Even on the hottest days, men in the frontline trenches had to keep a constant watch on the enemy. Any change in his routine was noted as it might signal an impending attack. As time went on, the habits of the foe became as well-known as those of a close friend. In one trench at Cape Helles, for example, the Ottomans daily watched the English exercising their horses, while 'another typical picture was the many small early morning clouds of smoke where the enemy prepared morning coffee'.[38] Both sights offered tempting targets but the Ottomans were forbidden to shoot due to their shortage of ammunition. They remained 'silent spectators', occasionally shaking their clenched fists in frustration.

Like so many problems on Gallipoli, the ammunition shortage was common to both sides although neither knew fully of the other's dilemma. 'There was plenty of infantry ammunition', Liman von Sanders writes, 'but artillery ammunition was inadequate from the beginning. As there were no efficient artillery ammunition factories in Constantinople and as neutral countries would not permit the passage of German ammunition, the Turkish batteries had to economise ammunition from the beginning of the battles . . . In the spring, Captain Pieper (German Navy) established an artillery ammunition factory in Constantinople; the relief was slight because neither the machines nor the materials were of the proper standard.'[39]

This shortage of suitable guns and ammunition saved the warriors from being exposed to the gigantic artillery duels that dominated warfare on the Western Front and sent many men mad with shell shock. The Ottomans were so short of artillery that antique guns were requisitioned from the Army Museum in İstanbul. 'Hundred year old mortars were installed in the front line to serve as trench mortars. However they harmed us more than the enemy, for their very thick, white clouds of smoke immediately attracted the enemy's fire. Our plea to have them reinstalled in the museum was heard.'[40] Items such as shovels and picks were also scarce and were much prized when captured from the Allies. Similarly, wood and iron for dugouts were scavenged from destroyed villages nearby.

We have several excellent accounts of what life was like for an Ottoman soldier on Gallipoli. One comes from a German colonel, Hans Kannengiesser, who served there most of the campaign. The book he wrote after the war reveals a genuine warmth towards the Ottoman and also displays a keen insight into the Turkish character.

Another important record is the recollections of Mustafa Yıldırım, a Turk who served briefly at Gallipoli. Let's explore what memories Mustafa has of his days as a soldier, and what Kannengiesser recalls of soldiers like Mustafa.

Most of the men under Kannengiesser's command 'came from

Ottoman troops from the 125th Regiment relax near Johnston's Jolly in what Zeki Bey called 'our most comfortable trenches'. The bearded, gowned man on the right is an imam (regimental chaplain). *AWM A02598*

Anatolia and Thrace and . . . [were] fairly well trained, brave, reliable and loyal; those from Anatolia were an overwhelming majority . . .'

[The Turkish soldier was] easily contented and modest, it did not even occur to him not to accept the authority of his superiors. He followed his leader unconditionally, also ahead into the enemy. Allah wills it. He is deeply religious and sees his life as the first step to a better one. Directly under the detonating grenades, shortly before the battalion enters a fight, the Imam, the army chaplain, normally delivers an address. The impression gained is always a strange one, particularly when, at the appropriate moments, one can hear an 'Inshallah' (may Allah grant it) from many hundreds of deep male voices resound solemnly across the wastelands. One evening, the jackals were howling already, I found the address rather long. The battalion was urgently needed at the front. However, I was careful not to interfere. It would have been ill received from a Christian. The Imams were often splendid people, who had a great and good influence on the men and would take up a command, if all officers had fallen, even a command of a battalion . . .

When troops fail, it is probably due to the leaders . . . In the fight I often had the impression: the unit is a willing mass, but they are lacking leaders to give them purpose. Out of this willingness and absolute acceptance of the authority of the superior follows the extraordinarily great influence a leader can have on his inferiors, if he is good, energetic and purposeful and Turkish—but he must be Turkish . . . [41]

For the most part, claims Kannengiesser, 'the [fighting] troops were pure Turkish Muslim . . . The Christians and the Jews were recruited

A quiet moment in the Ottoman trenches. While some men pose for the camera, one fellow receives a haircut. Note that the soldier near the left (at the rear) is barefoot. Seats and sleeping holes have been cut into the trenchside to make life a little bit more bearable. *AWM H13569*

GALLIPOLI

into work battalions or were used in other ways behind the front.'[42] These non-Muslim Ottoman subjects were almost all Greeks, Armenians or Ottoman Jews.

Kannengiesser was highly impressed by the Ottomans' frugal ways and simple dignity.

> From his youth he is used to sleeping on the hard floor. The Turks do not know the bed at all, at most they use carpets or mattresses which are taken from the cupboard at night and placed somewhere on the floor . . .
> Rice and meat are a luxury for him. The emergency ration, if there is one at all, consists of a slice of bread and some olives, the latter wrapped in the corner of a rather dubious looking handkerchief. In the morning he has gruel, late in the afternoon he has another soup, sometimes with meat, but always prepared with oil. His basic dish is Bulgur . . . squashed wheat cooked mostly in rancid oil and served cold.'[43]

One soldier remarked to Kannengiesser: ' "This is not a real war, since we are getting food every day." They probably had dreadful memories from the Balkan Wars, when they actually had to fill their bellies with grass, and feared hunger more than the enemy's bullet.'[44]

One thing that had not improved was the quality of the uniforms supplied to the troops. Kannengiesser writes: 'Clothing of the troops was incredible, even though we were only at the beginning of the war—summer and winter cloth mixed colourfully, torn and tattered. Footwear was quite varied, often only a piece of hide held together by a string. Often string had to replace leather in relation to equipment. Later on one saw a lot of English clothing.'[45] Whenever new supplies of sandbags arrived to rebuild the trenches, a large number always mysteriously went missing only to reappear later as patches on the men's clothing.

Generally speaking, Kannengiesser's men enjoyed relatively good health. 'In three battalions scurvy cropped up because of the sameness of the food; as we know today, because of its lacking in vitamins. I received fifty Turkish pounds from the Marshall [Liman von Sanders] and was thus able to buy fresh vegetables for those troops from Asia Minor. Combined with medical treatment this had a favourable effect. Otherwise we remained free from epidemics.'[46]

A medical complaint common among the Turks which greatly

annoyed Kannengiesser was 'teptil hawa' or 'change of climate disease'.

> Formerly . . . recruits doing their military service . . . had to serve
> in . . . distant areas of the [Ottoman] Empire. At that time, for example,
> people from the mountainous, healthy highland of Anatolia were sent to
> the fiercely hot area of Salonika. Many fell ill in the unfamiliar climate,
> especially during the hot season. They had to be granted home leave for
> months, if they were not to die. Nowadays, however, people . . . were
> enlisted in their home district. Nevertheless the doctors increasingly
> certified the necessity of such a change in climate. Of course, these 'teptil
> hawa' then aimed at prolonging their leave, once they were home, by fair or
> foul means. They never returned to their unit in time, often not at all.
> In this way the 'teptil hawa' unobtrusively slid into the class of deserters.[47]

Many of these troops were suffering from what we call 'home sickness'. The break from their family and village was especially painful for those who could not read or write. The vast majority of Ottomans in this period received no formal schooling and could neither write nor read letters. As there was no national telephone system, an illiterate soldier and his family often had no way of communicating with each other. A means was devised, however, to soften this heartache:

> The soldier's connection with his home was not, as otherwise usual, made
> by letter through the postal system, but mostly through an older man, who
> decided to visit the troops in the field. He would travel around in his area to
> collect letters and oral messages from parents and relatives. Then he would
> visit the troops in the field. After many months he would find them, and
> would exchange letters and messages with the soldiers of his area. Only
> after some more months would he return home.[48]

One young soldier who longed for his family and village was Mustafa Yıldırım. He came from the village of Sarız, near Kayseri in central eastern Anatolia. It was a small farming community of about ninety-five households. The villagers raised sheep and grew a variety of crops. Mustafa was only fifteen years old when the war began yet he considered himself very much an adult as he already smoked and owned a hunting gun. He had never attended school as there was none in the village. He spent his days working in the fields with his father.

One day, he recalls, 'a party of soldiers came to my village with flags and drums'. Mustafa and several uncles enlisted along with almost every other eligible man in the area. His two younger brothers stayed at home as they were not yet fifteen, the minimum age for joining the army. Men volunteered in the belief they were fighting 'infidels come to destroy the Muslim people'. The recruits were sent first to Kayseri for training, then set out on the long march across Anatolia to the Gallipoli peninsula. Mustafa, like many of the men, had never before left his region of Anatolia and had little knowledge of the wider world. 'We had never heard of Australia then. I had never heard of the British either', he recalled many years later. 'We all believed it was the Greeks we were fighting against at Gallipoli.' The mistake was easy to make since, in terms of the politics of the region, the western Allies were invading the Ottoman Empire in support of the Greek cause.

With so many men away, the women of the village took on all the farming tasks in addition to their normal family and village responsibilities. 'Women took care of everything and did all the work . . . tilling the fields and looking after the animals', Mustafa comments. 'Women cultivated the land; women harvested; women took the wheat to the mill, they did all the work. They were very brave women.' Life was extremely hard, yet people still had to pay their taxes. Many also donated horses, cattle and sheep to help the national war effort.

On Gallipoli, Mustafa worked in the supply corps carrying ammunition, food and other loads up to the depots behind the front line. The supplies were transported on whatever was available—donkeys, horses, carts pulled by cattle, anything. Occasionally during a trip, Mustafa met a man from a village near his own and they would swap stories about home.

Mustafa hated Gallipoli. The battlefield, he recalls, was 'a terrible place. I couldn't count the dead. We were under very heavy fire . . . It was chaos. You wouldn't know who was who'. About a month after arriving there, Mustafa decided to go home. One day, he simply wandered off and kept walking. Along the way he met other soldiers who had also deserted or were on leave. The trek home took almost a month. Once back in Sarız, 'some women . . . did make fun of me because I escaped' but the army never came after him.

Sarız, like villages across Anatolia, suffered great losses during the war. 'The villages were emptied of men. Of the eighty who went from my village . . . seventy-five were lost. We never heard of them again. Around Gallipoli the villages were totally deserted.' Several of Mustafa's uncles died at the war. Young Mustafa resumed farming with his father. Many, many years later, he and his wife moved to Australia. 'When I came here', Mustafa reflected when interviewed in the early 1980s, 'and found Australians had been fighting us in Gallipoli I didn't feel angry because it was so long ago. I am happy in Australia. But even if they gave me all of Australia, I still wouldn't give Australia a handful of my country'.[49]

Mustafa Yıldırım's and Hans Kannengiesser's stories tell us much about the difficulties the Ottoman people, both in the army and back in the villages, laboured under during 1915. In some respects (such as inferior equipment and inadequate clothing) the Ottomans were markedly worse off than the Allied soldiers. In other regards (water especially), conditions in the Ottoman trenches were more bearable than on the other side. The one thing soldiers from both sides would agree on was that after spending even a few weeks on Gallipoli, they would rather have been somewhere else . . . probably anywhere else but amidst the heat, the flies, the corpses and the dangers that confronted them every day on this most inhospitable peninsula. Mustafa Kemal spoke for every soldier in Gallipoli's trenches when years later he recalled of this time: 'I have been ill from breathing air of dead, putrefied bodies.'[50]

# FIVE

# *Honour is restored*

While the soldiers slogged it out on Gallipoli, life went on much as normal in İstanbul. Censorship of the press was so tight that, as always seems the case in such circumstances, rumours were endemic. One minute a person might be told the Ottomans had smashed the Allied army; the next minute the very opposite story was heard. The Ottoman press was strictly controlled and, as all newsprint paper came from Germany, the Germans made sure it went only to those newspaper proprietors who supported them. As might be expected, the Ottoman authorities made the most of every victory and minimised any defeat. Thus, when the initial Allied landings were contained, the Ottoman Minister for War boldly announced that the enemy had been defeated. Victory flags were hung in İstanbul's main streets and squares, and the sultan was invested with the title *Gazi* (the Victor) at a ceremony in the magnificent Ayasofya (St Sophia) mosque.

Even after it was clear that the celebrations had been rather premature, life in the Ottoman capital went on much as before. The rich still ate at their fashionable restaurants and the city's famous Pera Palace Hotel continued to accept guests. Only when a British submarine sank a supply ship anchored in the Golden Horn in late May 1915 did the citizens of İstanbul appreciate how real and how near the war actually was. It was not long before military authorities were deliberately transporting the long lines of wounded soldiers at night through deserted streets rather than allow the civilian populace to see the reality of war.

At the front, the stalemate dragged on. Early in June, British and

French infantry units launched yet another attack on Krithia which, for a few hours, forced the Ottomans to desert their front line trenches. The situation was soon retrieved, however, and the losses reclaimed. The armies hammered away relentlessly, but every Allied attack drew spirited defence so no effective gains were made. The casualty toll grew higher each day. Between 28 June and 5 July, for example, Ottoman losses around Cape Helles were estimated at 16 000 men.

Political leaders on both sides expected their generals to win them victories. When these did not come, tempers boiled and relations between the Ottoman and German officers soured somewhat. On the other side, some Australians and New Zealanders began to question the quality of the British leadership.

Ironically, the continued lack of success encouraged the generals of both armies to believe their defensive lines were quite secure when, in fact, the defences were far from perfect. Mustafa Kemal knew only too well that the northern section of the Ottoman line at Arı Burnu (around Sazlı Dere) was badly deficient in its defences. On quiet nights he and his regimental officers sometimes played war games on their maps. Each game only confirmed Kemal's belief that the area

Mustafa Kemal (fourth from the left) stands with a group of his Ottoman officers. *AWM P01141.001*

was dangerously undermanned. His fellow officers thought the section insignificant, but Kemal was convinced it gave the enemy a chance to push the Ottomans aside and capture the dominating peaks, Chunuk Bair and Koca Çimen Tepe (Hill 1971). Once established on these high points, the Allies would be poised to gain control of the entire region and thus force the straits. Week after week, Kemal pestered his superiors on the matter but no-one listened. He twice resigned in protest on the issue but Liman von Sanders persuaded him to return.

Kemal's petulance was but one of the many problems von Sanders had to face. In late July, rumours circulated that the Allies were preparing another great offensive. Reports reached Ottoman Headquarters that thousands of fresh Allied troops were gathering on Lemnos Island. While von Sanders prepared to meet the expected attack, an order came from German High Command in Berlin instructing him to return immediately to Germany, as a new commander was arriving to replace him. Apparently, some senior Ottoman politicians who disagreed with his battle strategy had engineered his removal. The recall was strategically suicidal at so critical a moment in the campaign. It was also a deep personal insult. Incensed, von Sanders despatched a long telegram on 28 July seeking clarification of the order. Two days later he was told the recall had been deferred. Nothing more was ever heard of the matter.

Rumours of new landings were now circulating freely. It could have done von Sanders's confidence no good to be informed by a visiting officer 'that the success of this new enterprise was counted on with such certainty [in İstanbul] that already windows were being rented in Pera Street for the entry of the British troops and that the British Embassy was being put in order and the beds newly covered. I [von Sanders] merely replied that I requested him to order a window for me too in Pera Street.'[1]

The gossip was well founded. Frustrated by the lack of progress being made by their armies in France, the British war lords had decided to devote more resources to the Mediterranean campaign. 'Constantinople is the prize, and the only prize which lies within reach this year', Winston Churchill pronounced. 'It can certainly be won without unreasonable expense, and within a comparatively

Recruiting campaigns in Australia during 1915 drew heavily on the Gallipoli theme. To some degree, similar artistic devices are used in the 1916 Syrian presentation rug reproduced as this book's endpapers. H.M. Burton, *A call from the Dardanelles* . . . 100 × 47 cm. *AWM ARTV05167*

short time. But we must act now, and on a scale which makes speedy success certain.'[2] Three fresh divisions were despatched, bringing the effective strength of Hamilton's army to 120 000 men.

These new units were to assist in a major offensive planned for early August. Hamilton had finally decided that his policy of hammering away at Cape Helles was futile; he now intended shifting his major focus to the Sarı Bayır ridge, just north of the Anzac lines. The Australian historian, Alan Moorehead, sums up the plan thus:

He proposed to break out of the north of the Anzac bridgehead by night and assault Chunuk Bair and the crest of the hills, having first made a major feint at a place called Lone Pine in the south. Simultaneously there was to be a new landing at Suvla Bay, immediately to the north of Anzac, and it was hoped that as soon as the hills there were taken the combined force would push through to the Narrows about four miles [six-and-a-half kilometres] away. With the bulk of the Turkish Army then bottled up in the tip of the peninsula, and under heavy pressure from the French and the British at Cape Helles, it was hoped that there would be a quick ending to the campaign.[3]

The scheme bore many similarities to the 25 April attack, being a multi-pronged assault which depended, above all, on surprise. It strove to lure the Ottomans into over-committing their forces at one point then hitting them even harder at another. If things went to plan and a breakthrough made, the Ottoman supply lines would soon falter (or so the Allied generals believed) and the stranded Ottoman armies would quickly crumble, thus opening the way for the Allies to seize the straits. British and French warships could then steam up the Dardanelles and take İstanbul.

Several criticisms can be made of the plan. First, it rather underestimated the Ottomans' powers to counterattack, even though the Allies had very accurate information on Ottoman troop numbers and knew only too well their opponent's uncanny ability to organise quick, effective counterattacks. Second, the plan assumed that once driven off the high ground, Ottoman resistance would quickly fold. The Allies' own experience should have made them realise that a determined foe could still put up a determined fight even when in an inferior position. Finally, each part of the ambitious plan depended very heavily on the success of the other attacks—if any one phase failed (in particular, the assault on Chunuk Bair), the entire advance was most probably doomed.

The Ottomans were reasonably well placed to meet any new offensive on Gallipoli. Their army now comprised about 500 000 men, 110 000 of whom were in the Gallipoli region. Their relations with neighbouring Bulgaria were improving but an army was still positioned near that border for safety. The situation on the Eastern Front and around Suez and Mesopotamia was stable so, except for watching Bulgaria, all efforts could be turned to Gallipoli.

Von Sanders's intelligence sources had been unable to discover where or when the Allies' attack would occur. The German general guessed that a new force might be landed between Hell Spit and Cape Helles, so Colonel Kannengiesser's 9th Division was moved into this gap. Each side had roughly equal numbers of men at the front (Allies 120 000; the Ottomans 110 000) but they were deployed very differently. By 6 August, the Allies had increased their forces in and around Anzac Cove from 16 000 to 37 000. Ottoman infantry strength in the area was about 21 000.

Ottoman soldiers outside the entrace to a tunnel at Kanlı Sırt. The man nearest the camera is holding several small handbombs. Note, too, the patches on his colleague's trousers. *AWM A02599*

At 2 p.m. on 6 August, three mines exploded in front of the Ottoman lines at Lone Pine, towards the southern end of the Anzac zone. Explosions of this type occurred frequently and caused only moderate alarm. The Ottoman troops were not to know that the blasts were a softening-up blow at the commencement of the much vaunted new offensive. Two hours later, British ships began bombarding Cape Helles and several hundred Greek troops made a dummy landing in the north of the peninsula. At about the same time, British troops charged towards Krithia in yet another diversionary attack. The Ottoman guns replied with such ferocity that nearly 2000 of the 3000 British troops engaged were wounded.

The Ottoman lines at Lone Pine came under heavy bombardment at 4.30 p.m. Luckily, several deep mining tunnels connected with the trenches so most of the 500 troops in the front line moved into this underground shelter. The pounding kept up for an hour. Then, whistles were heard and Australians poured forth towards the opposing line. 'Look out. The English are coming', shouted one Turk. A sergeant rushed to the tunnels to summon his men as those few troops already in position opened fire on the advancing Aussies. The fire increased quickly as more men clambered to the surface, but the attackers were upon them before the defence could be properly coordinated.

The Ottomans had roofed their front trenches with heavy pine logs covered with sand. Where gaps remained, the Australians jumped into the trench and fought hand to hand with the defenders. Elsewhere, Australian rifles were poked through the roof and fired indiscriminately into the gloom below. Other Australians ran beyond the trenches to tackle the men in nearby supporting positions. About seventy Ottomans were taken prisoner as they emerged from their tunnels.

Esad Paşa, the senior Ottoman general, had his headquarters overlooking Lone Pine. He grasped the seriousness of the attack immediately: his artillery quickly opened fire and reinforcements were despatched at once. Major Zeki Bey led this relief force. In 1919, he recounted the events to the Australian historian CEW Bean:

> From the regimental headquarters at the back of Mortar Ridge you could see clearly. There was a lot of dust raised by the shells at Kanlı Sırt [Lone

Pine]. I could not see through it, but when the bombardment there ceased we heard infantry fire—like after thunder you hear the rain beginning; and the observers beside us said, 'the English are getting into our trenches'.

Our observation of this bombardment had given us the impression that the trenches subjected to it would not be in a condition to repel the attack—there had been much damage, and heavy loss. At that moment an order arrived by telephone lines from Mustafa Kemal Paşa: . . . the battalion of reserve . . . will move at once to 'Kanlı Sırt'. The battalion was ready to go. I gave the order to move as fast as possible . . . On the way, we fixed bayonets . . .

The moment we turned into that valley we came into fire, from your men at the head of it . . . Near there I met the commander of one of the battalions which had been holding the centre of the Kanlı Sırt front . . . I asked, 'What has happened?' But he was clearly very shocked. He kept on saying, 'We're lost, we're lost!'

I said, 'I want you to tell me what the situation is and what you wish me to do.'

He said: 'The situation is critical. My whole battalion remained in shelter of the trenches after the bombardment. I'm waiting here for the remnants of it—I have no one now under my command. If any survive, I'm here to stop them and take them under my command.'

But there was no one there except him. I saw it was useless to ask for information from him, and I didn't want to lose time . . .[4]

Local units were already stemming the Australian advance. In one trench, a 'brave cool-headed' priest rallied men to the defence. Zeki Bey quickly organised a new defensive line. Heavy machine gun fire and brilliant flares kept up well into the night. '[T]here was great confusion and disorder in the valley and the trenches', Zeki Bey remembered.[5]

It was now the turn of the Australians at Lone Pine to look down the gully upon the enemy lines. For the next three days, the Ottomans sniped, bombed and charged the Lone Pine trenches. Neither side would yield a fraction of the now bloody soil. 'On the third day', states Zeki Bey, 'I sent a company to attack and it disappeared altogether; I don't know if it was captured or killed . . .'[6] The counter-attack was finally called off on 9 August when the men were too exhausted to attempt another charge. Just how many lives were lost will never be known exactly. Most estimates set the tally at well over 6000 Ottomans and 2300 Australians.

MAJOR ZEKI BEY.
COMMANDANT OF TURKISH REGIMENT
AT GALLIPOLI.

Major Zeki Bey, as drawn by the Australian war artist George Lambert in February 1919, when an Australian historical mission returned to the Gallipoli battlefields. Zeki Bey served as guide to the Australians. Pencil 30.2 × 22.5 cm. *AWM ART02868*

The sights and smells of death were all around. One Australian wrote in his diary:

[Bodies] were lying everywhere, on top of the parapet . . . in dugouts and communication trenches and saps; and it was impossible to avoid treading on them. In the second line the Turkish dead were lying everywhere, and if a chap wanted to sit down for a spell he was often compelled to squat on one of 'em.[7]

Nobody who saw the scene could ever again regard war as glorious. One shocked Australian who visited the trenches on 7 August wrote of what surrounded him:

> Right beside me, within a space of fifteen feet [four-and-a-half metres], I can count fourteen of our boys stone dead. Ah! it is a piteous sight. Men and boys who yesterday were full of joy and life, now lying there, cold— cold—dead—their eyes glassy, their faces sallow and covered with dust—soulless—gone—somebody's son, somebody's boy—now merely a thing. Thank God that their loved ones cannot see them now—dead, with the blood congealed or oozing out. God, what a sight. The major is standing next to me and he says 'Well we have won.' Great God—won— what means a victory and all those bodies within arms' reach—then may I never witness a defeat.[8]

As after previous slaughters, the hot sun soon putrefied the corpses. The diary entry for 9 August of one soldier read:

> The stench of the dead bodies now is simply awful, as they have been fully exposed to the sun for several days, many have swollen terribly and have burst . . . many men wear gas protectors . . . there has been no attempt up to the present to either remove or bury [the dead], they are stacked out of the way in any convenient place sometimes thrown up on to the parados so as not to block the trenches, there are now more dead than living . . .[9]

Even when in the thick of the action at Lone Pine, Zeki Bey could not help noticing the heavy fighting going on elsewhere in Anafartalar. 'All these days', he later said, 'I was looking over my shoulder at the Anzac shells bursting on the reverse slope of Chunuk Bair, and, although the situation at Lone Pine was critical, I could scarcely keep my eyes on it. I knew that things must be happening on Chunuk Bair which were more important by far.'[10] The Ottoman High Command, despite Kemal's warnings, had always believed the extremely rugged country just north of Arı Burnu made it 'quite impracticable for troops in formation'. Thus, only small garrison units guarded these steep peaks and gullies. Zeki Bey could sense that something had gone very wrong up there.

Chunuk Bair was a central peak in the Sari Bair range running behind and to the north of the Anzac battlezone. It and Hill 971 had not been directly threatened since the initial landings and thus had been left unmanned, thereby allowing seemingly more precarious points to be defended. The Allies knew this and believed the hills might be captured by a surprise night attack. These attacks were the centrepiece of the great August offensive.

At 9 p.m. on 6 August, as bitter fighting continued in the recently exchanged trenches at Lone Pine, a heavy barrage hit the Ottoman positions north of Anzac Cove. During the night, New Zealand, Australian and Indian units pushed inland towards Hill 971 (Koca Çimen Tepe). At first, they met only isolated groups of Ottomans who quickly retired. Later on, however, the pockets of resistance grew much stronger. This, plus the difficult terrain and the darkness, caused all the advancing units to fall behind schedule. None had reached its objective by dawn. The New Zealanders were closest— a thousand metres from Chunuk Bair and two-and-a-half kilometres from Hill 971. They stopped for breakfast unaware that, at the moment, they outnumbered the Ottomans in the area by a factor of ten to one.

Throughout the night, the Ottoman commanders were unsure exactly what was happening. Mustafa Kemal, for example, heard the artillery fire but could not locate the battle. At 3.30 a.m., he issued the rather general order:

> It is probable that the enemy will attack our front in the morning. Owing to the close distance and in order to be able to repel at once any sudden attacks, it is essential that troops are awake and the men ready to use their weapons. Therefore I request officers to encourage the men to keep awake and maintain the highest degree of readiness at all times . . .[11]

Once morning arrived, the major thrust of the attack was easier to locate. Kemal immediately despatched his only reserves to defend Chunuk Bair. Meanwhile, Colonel Kannengiesser's 9th Division was summoned, arriving just in time to repulse the Allied drive towards Hill 971. Once again, the Ottoman defence had held fast, but the crisis was still far from over.

Early in the morning of 7 August, the Australians made another four feint attacks. Each was repulsed. One of them, the charge at the

Nek, is especially remembered for its futility. The Australian attackers were meant to be supported by a naval bombardment right up until the time they raced across the twenty metres stretch of no-man's land to the Ottoman line but, due to a mix-up, the shelling stopped seven minutes early. The Ottoman soldiers cautiously crept from their shelters and aimed their machine guns and rifles at the Anzac parapet.

As soon as heads appeared above the trench, they unleashed a massive barrage of bullets. Few of the attackers got even five metres and only one or two reached the Ottoman line. In the next forty-five minutes, three more lines of Australians leapt up to virtually certain death. It was 19 May all over again, only this time the roles were reversed. Legend has it that some Ottoman machine gunners climbed out of their trenches and sat on the parapet to get a clearer shot. According to the Australian historian Bill Gammage, by 5.15 a.m., 'two hundred and thirty-five [Australian] lighthorsemen lay in an area little larger than a tennis court. Most were still there in 1919, their bones whitening the ridges to observers half a mile [800 metres] away'.[12]

As the Australians fell at the Nek, English troops at Suvla Bay (several kilometres north and clearly visible from trenches at the Nek) were cooking breakfast. The Suvla force was a key element in Hamilton's plan. Fresh landings were made at Suvla Bay from where the troops would advance inland between three and seven kilometres to capture several small hills not occupied by the Ottomans. This would secure the northern approaches to Sari Bair and, it was hoped, might even stretch Ottoman resources to breaking point. Great care was taken to mask preparations for these new landings which consequently came as a complete surprise to the defenders.

The Suvla area was defended by a tiny force of 1500 Ottoman *jandarma* (military police) led by a Bavarian, Major Willmer. When the British started to disembark along the flat Suvla beaches during the night of 6–7 August, all that the greatly outnumbered defenders could do was harass and harry. Their snipers and artillery were so effective that the British showed great reluctance to advance. The Ottomans slowly retired to some nearby foothills that gave them a full view of any British advance across the plains.

Things were so chaotic back at headquarters that von Sanders did not learn of the Suvla landings until late in the afternoon of 7 August. The news made it clear that Chunuk Bair and Hill 971, not Bulair, were the British objectives. Accordingly, von Sanders immediately ordered every available soldier on the Asiatic side of the Dardanelles to cross to the peninsula; the 8th Division at Krithia to march north to Anzac, and the 7th and 12th Divisions to march down from Bolayir [Bulair], over 40 kilometres further up the peninsula. It would take between thirty-six and forty-eight hours for these reinforcements to arrive. In the meantime, local units would have to repel the attack as best they could.

Willmer's force performed magnificently. Its spirited defence so worried the timid British commanders that their 20 000 men dug in rather than advance against only 1500 defenders. High up on Chunuk Bair, Kannengiesser watched in amazement: 'Suvla Bay was full of ships. We counted ten transports, six warships and seven hospital ships. On land we saw a confused mass of troops like a disturbed ant-heap. Nowhere was there fighting in progress.'[13] At 7 p.m. on 7 August, Willmer reported that although thousands of British troops had been put ashore that day, 'the enemy is advancing timidly'. Late in the day some British units did push inland and captured several highpoints but the gains cost them 1600 men and 100 officers, more than the entire Ottoman force there!

By the evening of 7 August, the defence of the entire peninsula hung in the balance. The defenders at Suvla and Arı Burnu were hard pressed yet reinforcements were still many hours march away. Reports reaching Mustafa Kemal showed that some officers were confused and panicky. 'Everything is in a muddle. The situation is serious', one reported. 'No officers can be found . . . I do not even know of the place where I am', another admitted.[14] Kemal sent out a junior officer to Chunuk Bair to report back personally, but he was killed.

Very early next morning, some New Zealanders pushed up Chunuk Bair and established themselves on its crest. This offered a glimpse of the Narrows—the first time since 25 April they could be seen from the Anzac lines. The Kiwis were pounded so hard by the Ottomans that, by the day's end, only seventy of the 760 men who began the attack were not wounded. An early morning attempt by the Australians to push ahead towards Hill 971 was turned back by 'an inferno' of shells and rifle fire. The Anzacs suffered 750 casualties. Elsewhere, the fire slackened during the day, except at Lone Pine where the Ottomans continued to attack *en masse*. Miraculously, Willmer's small force was still holding the line at Suvla.

Von Sanders had been assured that the two divisions from Bulair would reach Suvla late on 7 August, but when dawn broke on 8 August, the reinforcements still had not arrived. Their commanding officer, Ahmed Fevzi Bey, then claimed his men were too tired from the long march to attack before sunset. Besides, he contended, none of his officers were familiar with the terrain so any attack should be delayed until some preparations were made. Fevzi later asked that the attack again be postponed to the following morning. Von Sanders would abide such excuses no longer and dismissed him on the spot. An officer at Helles was also dismissed for showing insufficient resolve to fight. Later that night, von Sanders telephoned Kemal.

> 'What is your opinion of the present situation?' the general asked.
> 'Very critical', replied Kemal. 'We still have a little time left to us to save it, but if we do not use our moment we shall lose everything. Conditions on the whole front are chaotic. The enemy is still landing men in the Suvla area.'
> 'What can be done to save the situation?'
> 'We must unite all the commands under one commander.'
> 'Is there no alternative?'
> 'No. No alternative. You must place all the forces under my command.'
> 'But surely they are too many', remarked von Sanders.
> 'Too few', replied Kemal and hung up.[15]

The strong will and straight talking of the man impressed the German general immensely. He quickly consulted with other senior officers who agreed that Mustafa Kemal should lead the attack. Kemal was instructed immediately to assume command of the Anafartalar sector. The Turkish colonel set off at 11.30 p.m. to take up his new post. The night ride was blissful relaxation after the great strain of recent days. 'The battle', he recalled later, 'had compelled me to be three days and three nights without sleep and perpetually

Liman von Sanders (left) with Mustafa Kemal.

on duty. I was really in an ill condition. In fact, the bloody fighting which had lasted for three or four months on the Arı Burnu front had tired me out to such an extent and made me so thin that . . . [even without] the fatigue of these last days, I would still have been in an ill condition.'[16] Nevertheless, he conferred all night with his new officers and decided to launch a counterattack immediately.

Hamilton had, by now, travelled to Suvla to oversee personally the offensive and ensure that a more aggressive approach be adopted. In the early hours of 9 August, the British were cautiously moving towards the vital high point Tekke Tepe (twelve kilometres north of Hill 971), when Kemal's offensive swept over them. The Ottoman artillery and machine gun fire was so intense, it ignited the scrub. The British lines broke into panic and ran. By mid-morning they had regrouped in the middle of the plain, but the advantage now lay firmly with Kemal. When Kemal recounted these dramatic days to a journalist in 1918, his recollections were less than complimentary towards his opponents:

> ... when Ottoman soldiers attacked ferociously, supported by accurate shrapnel fire from mountain batteries, the 'English' soldiers could only think of escaping towards the sea. I was surprised to hear later that even General Ian Hamilton came on location and could not have his commands obeyed and there was much discussion and procrastination amongst the senior officers. This allowed us to win ... We captured many machine guns and prisoners.[17]

'At Chunuk Bair, in the meantime', recalls an Ottoman officer, 'nothing important had been done. Mustafa Kemal Paşha [sic], who had been given control there, was directing the Anafarta [sic] attack. The situation at Chunuk Bair was very critical because Esad Paşa had no more troops.'[18] Kemal rode back to Chunuk Bair in the afternoon. The Allies had made good their foothold near the summit and the Ottomans were gradually wilting under a heavy naval bombardment. Kemal reasoned that the time had come to launch an all-out attack with every available man. His officers protested that their men were now too weak, but Kemal insisted he be obeyed. The attack was set for daylight next morning.

Folklore has it that Kemal crept out into no-man's land a few minutes before the start-time. 'Don't hurry. Let me go first', he had instructed his men. 'Wait until you see me raise my whip and then all rush forward together.'[19] At 4.30 a.m., he gave the signal and his men swarmed down on the British lines. The Allies were swept from their trenches and chased down the seaward slopes. Thousands of Ottomans were cut down by rifle fire and naval artillery shells but the heights were again theirs. During the battle, a piece of shrapnel hit Kemal on the right side of his chest. Luckily for him, it struck the watch in his shirt pocket. Kemal later presented his shattered watch as a souvenir to Liman von Sanders who, in turn, gave him his wrist watch.

The massive effort of the past four days had taken a terrible toll on both armies. The Allies lost between 12 000 and 13 000 men. Ottoman losses were even higher: 9200 men on Chunuk Bair and Hill 971; between 1800 and 2000 around Baby 700; and almost 7000 at Lone Pine. Practically every point in the Ottoman line had been threatened at some time or other during the offensive. Thus, it was with much relief that one of von Sanders's senior officers could write in his diary: 'On the evening of the tenth all the heights, with the exception of the insignificant elevation of Chocolate Hill [on Suvla plain], are firmly in the hands of the Turks.'[20]

Over 400 Ottomans and several Germans were taken prisoner by the Allies during the four days. They were led down to Anzac Cove and held in a large barbed wire pen specially built for the offensive. Indian sentries stood guard over them, although they need hardly have bothered, for the enclosure was invariably surrounded by curious Anzacs. The history books do not tell us what happened

A work party of Ottoman prisoners of war and their guards at Anzac Cove enjoy a break from the job. *AWM G00456*

to these prisoners. Presumably, they were shipped off to spend the rest of the war at POW camps in Egypt.

The Kemal-inspired counterattacks of 9 and 10 August had, in reality, settled the fate of the Allies' second offensive. But Hamilton and his generals kept battering away in the vain hope that some advantage might still be got. They launched another three major attacks around Suvla in August, none of which materially altered the front line. The assaults worried von Sanders, nevertheless, forcing him to call up the last of his reserves and thus leave the Asiatic coast and the northern section of the peninsula virtually unprotected. Fortunately for the Ottomans, the Allies knew nothing of his dilemma—not that they could do much about it.

The August offensive broke the spirit of the Allied armies. They had thrown everything they could muster at the Ottomans but the resistance had not collapsed and no major breakthroughs were achieved. The Ottomans too, were weary, and both sides entered a convalescence period rather like the slowdown in fighting after the massive May attacks.

After the August battles, the respect felt by the opposing troops for each other developed, in many cases, into what can only be called friendships. The Allies referred fondly to the enemy as 'Johnny Turk'; the Ottoman troops called the British soldiers 'John Kikrik' and the French 'Tango'. These men had shared the same agonies, privations and boredom for so long that many now regarded the troops opposite them more as companions in adversity than mortal enemies. Thus, one Australian wrote home in a letter:

> We got an interpreter up, and he sang out to [the Ottomans] . . . and finally got about a dozen . . . up on the parapet having a 'yap' to him—and one of our chaps went over and got a cigarette case from them . . .
>
> When we want to send a note over we 'ring them up' by knocking a stone on a tin periscope—and they answer by waving a periscope. Then if the note gets into their trench alright, they give another wave as an acknowledgement.[21]

Some British troops helped the Turks celebrate the end of the Muslim Ramadan festival by throwing over gifts of food. Incidents like these became increasingly common, especially around the Anzac area where no-man's land was so narrow. One day at Quinn's Post, for example:

> a note was thrown over by the Turks, evidently in answer to one from our chaps asking the distance to Constantinople . . .'You ask how far it is to Constantinople. How long will you please be in getting there?' They used a knife as a weight when they threw the note and asked for it to be returned. It was thrown back but fell short . . . On being told where it was they asked our chaps not to fire while one of them got it . . . On another occasion there must have been a German officer approaching, for all of a sudden the Turks began signalling to our chaps to get down in their trenches. They immediately took the hint and then a machine gun began to play along the parapet from end to end. Of course, no damage was done. This shows something of the fairness with which the Turk fights.[22]

Impromptu shooting matches were arranged, Ottoman and Anzac taking it in turns to fire at a target held above the enemy lines. Scores were exchanged and, on occasion, bets made for bully beef or the like.

Fraternisation was not without its risks, however. An Australian joker might shout out: 'Hello Turk.' 'Hello Australia', would come the reply. 'How many of you are in [i.e. will share] a tin of bully?' 'Oh Tousand. Tousands.' 'Well, divide that among you', yelled the Anzac lobbing over a home-made bomb.[23] The Ottomans played much the same game. Another Australian's letter home asked the question:

> Did I ever tell you of Ernest? Ernest was a gaunt old Turk who used to come out of his trench every morning to gather firewood (our chaps never fired a shot for a long while). They used to chuck him tins of bully and he'd salaam and thank them. Poor old Ernest died a sudden death one morning when a new lot came in the trenches.[24]

During November the Anzacs began compiling their own book, something akin to a school magazine. About 150 troops submitted material. Their stories, drawings and photos were published in 1916 as *The Anzac Book*. Several of the contributions refer respectfully or in good-natured fun to 'Johnny Turk' or his servant 'Beachy Bill' (a gun sited behind Gaba Tepe which regularly shelled the Anzac area). A page of frivolous advertisements in the book includes the following:

NOTICE—The Turkish artillery is requested to refrain from wasting ammunition whilst our meals are being served . . .
WANTED—Fifty thousand Turkish prisoners for wharf-lumping, road-making, and building officers' dugouts. Plenty of permanent work for men of right stamp. Apply any beach fatigue party—Australian N.Z. Army Corps.[25]

In a more serious vein was the poem, 'Abdul', written by the Australian press correspondent and editor of *The Anzac Book*, C.E.W. Bean:

We've drunk the boys who rushed the hills,
    The men who stormed the beach,
The sappers and the A.S.C.,
    We've had a toast for each;
And the guns and stretcher-bearers—
    But, before the bowl is cool,
There's one chap I'd like to mention,
    He's a fellow called ABDUL.

We haven't seen him much of late—
    Unless it be his hat,
Bobbing down behind a loophole . . .
    And we mostly blaze at that;
But we hear him wheezing there at nights,
    Patrolling through the dark,
With his signals—hoots and chirrups—
    Like an early morning lark.

We've heard the twigs a-crackling,
    As we crouch upon the knees,
And his big, black shape went smashing,
    Like a rhino, through the trees.
We've seen him fling in, rank on rank,
    Across the morning sky;
And we've had some pretty shooting,
    And—he knows the way to die.

Yes, we've seen him dying there in front—
    Our own boys died there, too—
With his poor dark eyes a-rolling,
    Staring at the hopeless blue;

With his poor maimed arms a-stretching
   To the God we both can name . . .
And it fairly tore our hearts out;
   But it's in the beastly game.

So though your name be black as ink
   For murder and rapine,
Carried out in happy concert
   With your Christians from the Rhine,
*We* will judge you, Mr Abdul,
   By the test by which *we* can—
That with all your breath, in life, in death,
   You've played the gentleman.[26]

The poem was accompanied by a painting presenting 'Abdul' probably as most Anzacs perceived him: a solid, slightly chubby man (suggesting the Anzacs believed the Ottomans were better fed than they were) with a swarthy complexion and shifty, slightly cruel expression on his face. His uniform and boots are worn and patched yet still look neat and he carries all his belongings in several small, tidy bags. The caricature is completed with the inevitable cigarette (Turkish?) jutting from the side of his mouth.

The commanders, of course, did not condone any fraternisation with the enemy. Who knew what might happen if the soldiers were allowed to become friendly towards each other!

In September and October, the strategic balance in the wider region tilted the Ottomans' way. Earlier in the year, their major ally, Germany, had inflicted a series of crushing defeats on Russia. These victories and the impressive Ottoman performance on Gallipoli were noted with great interest by those European countries not yet in the war. Both the Allied and Central Powers constantly sought to woo these non-aligned states. As 1915 progressed, it appeared that the tide of war in the Balkans and the East was flowing the Central Powers' way. On 6 September, previously non-aligned Bulgaria signed a pact with Austria–Hungary and Germany, and mobilised its armies before the month was out.

Bulgaria's action delighted Enver Paşa as it created the possibility of opening the railway from Berlin to İstanbul. This line

An Anzac's impression of his enemy, 'Abdul', produced
for *The Anzac Book*. Ted Colles, watercolour with pencil
29.5 × 22.2 cm. *AWM (46)*

passed through neutral Serbia and Bulgaria and hence had been
closed to the transportation of armaments and troops. If Bulgaria
and Serbia sided with Germany, the line would open and the
Ottomans could be reinforced with German troops and artillery.
But the Serbs refused to join, so early in October, Austro–German
and Bulgarian armies invaded her. The Allies transferred several
divisions from Gallipoli to Salonika to bolster the Serbian defence
but this force arrived too late to be of real assistance. The Serbian
campaign was over before November ended and the corridor from
Berlin to İstanbul fully open.

In reducing their Gallipoli forces, the Allies had aided the Ottomans enormously. King Constantine, the King of Greece and a brother-in-law of the Kaiser, interpreted the Allies' action as a sign that they were about to abandon Gallipoli, so he dismissed his anti-German prime minister and adopted a policy of strict neutrality. The Ottoman Empire's star, it seemed, was truly in the ascendant.

Late in August, the torturously hot summer at last began to fade. The nights grew decidedly cool in September and, in October, heavy autumn storms blew up. All too soon the intense summer heat seemed a pleasant memory to men now freezing in icy cold trenches. Efforts were made to improve the trenches against the fierce storms but it was impossible to keep out the cold and water.

The troops awoke on Sunday, 28 November to find the land-scape blanketed with snow. The temperature did not rise above freezing all day, making life even more miserable than normal. Fighting was again largely forgotten as everyone struggled to get warm. Small fires were lit in the trenches, but wood was very scarce. The Ottoman troops suffered most as the wind and snow blew into the backs of their lines and right into their dugouts. Some men actually died of frostbite. As the snow melted over the next few days, some trenches flooded, then froze. A few men drowned when their trench suddenly turned into a swirling stream.

As the year drew towards its end, the fighting, around Anafartalar and Suvla especially, was desultory. For days on end, the Allied guns did not let off a single shot and the Anzac troops fired only rarely. Some Ottoman officers suspected the enemy might be evacuating so, occasionally, raiding parties were sent out to check the Allies' front lines. The parties always met strong resistance, but only when they got very near the Anzac trenches.

Sensing that morale was crumbling within the Allies' ranks, von Sanders began planning 'a violent and extensive attack' to take place between Arı Burnu and Suvla. New reinforcements were assembled and experienced divisions removed from the line to train in practice trenches dug well away from the front. Berlin sent out special technical units to assist with these preparations. Security was so tight that the large consignments of ammunition being amassed were specially labelled with a cipher few could understand. Von Sanders hoped preparations would be finalised by late January. Many Ottomans were exasperated by the slowness of the preparations.

Shortly before dawn on 20 December, a large Allied mine was exploded at the Nek, killing nearly seventy Ottoman troops. The survivors braced themselves for action as, normally, such explosions preceded large infantry attacks. Minutes passed without a single head appearing above the Anzac parapet. It was considered standard practice in the Ottoman Army to seize any new craters immediately after a mine exploded. Thus, the company commander warily advanced his men in the early morning mist towards the craters. No-one opposed them. The explosion had been so great that one crater led into an Australian trench. The troops scurried in and found it empty. They reported this to their officer who confirmed it personally, then sent back the news to headquarters. Also about this time, fires were seen in the Allies' huge stacks of stores at Suvla. This was strange as the Ottoman artillery had not been shelling them. Clearly, peculiar things were happening within the Allies' lines. At 4.30 a.m., the Ottomans opposite Quinn's Post and nearby positions were ordered to advance on these positions. None met any resistance so, at about 7 a.m., an attack was launched against the entire Anzac line.

British warships were now shelling the peninsula, only this time their shells were mostly falling in and behind the Anzac trenches. The Ottomans advanced hesitantly, but when no-one came out to oppose them, they ran down the steep hillsides. The trenches were empty. The enemy had fled. Zeki Bey remembers that:

> At first only the [front] companies were ordered to advance; later the troops, some of them, went in without orders. On the first day they were everywhere. Stores abandoned . . . were ordered to be collected—sandbags and other material for the trenches were sent to our troops at Helles, but the soldiers at Anzac helped themselves to these very largely.[27]

The trenches seemed to have been vacated very recently as, in some instances, meals were laid out on tables ready for eating. The food had, in fact, been specially left by the Anzacs as a final act of friendship. Others were not so hospitable and had set booby traps such as oil stoves which exploded when lit or had smashed the contents of their dugout rather than allow the crude furniture to become 'a curiosity in some Turkish Officer's home'. 'Don't forget, Johnny, we left—you didn't push us off', read one message left behind.

Eighty-three thousand Allied soldiers had been evacuated from Anzac and Suvla with scarcely a casualty. The withdrawal was planned so masterfully, the Ottomans had no inkling that the forces opposite them had been steadily diminishing for the past four weeks. The deception was achieved by maintaining an appearance of absolute normality in trench life. It meant that enormous quantities of stores and equipment had to be left behind. Delighted Ottoman soldiers helped themselves to thousands of tins of biscuits, jam, meat, tea and sugar. All manner of things had been abandoned: five small steamboats, sixty rowboats, narrow gauge railways, telephone equipment, medical stores, ammunition dumps, row upon row of wagons, hundreds of tents. The list went on and on. For weeks after, Ottoman soldiers were walking around wearing odd mixtures of Ottoman, British and Australian uniforms, their knapsacks bulging with booty. A less pleasant discovery was the hundreds of horses slaughtered before the evacuation.

Ottoman troops stand triumphant on Anzac Beach after the Allied evacuation. Behind them are large water condensers and other items of equipment left behind by the retreating army. *AWM C03207*

The Ottomans down at Cape Helles were very critical of their northern comrades for allowing the enemy to escape so easily. Some historians have echoed this criticism. In defence of the local Ottoman forces, it must be stated that the Allies' preparations were so thorough, very little change could be detected from the Ottoman side without launching a major attack and neither side felt much inclination for that. 'No one regretted that we hadn't known of your intention to withdraw', Zeki Bey told an Australian years later.[28] Perhaps, in a strange way, the Ottoman troops thought it only proper that the enemy, though vanquished, was not humiliated.

Von Sanders ordered the troops to fortify the Anzac beaches just in case another landing was attempted. He transferred the best

This photograph reputedly shows Ottoman officers watching the Allied ships withdrawing from the seas around the Gallipoli peninsula in December 1915. One suspects it might have been taken at a later date as the group seems unusually relaxed. *AWM A05297*

available divisions to Cape Helles and instructed his commanders there to keep close watch for any unusual British activity. By the first week in January, clear evidence had been detected by ground and air spotters that men and equipment were being shipped out. Anxious to avoid a repeat of the Anzac evacuation, von Sanders ordered a major attack for 7 January. It opened with the heaviest bombardment of the entire campaign and the explosion of two large mines. The assault force met very stiff resistance when it sprang from the trenches; so stiff that follow-up units refused to charge. Their officers first shouted encouragement, then insults, but few men ventured into the open and near-certain death. The men, it seemed, sensed that the campaign was nearly over and thus had no desire to expose themselves to now unnecessary dangers. The attack fizzled out. Next day, Ottoman guns shelled the British trenches quite severely but no more infantry charges were attempted. That night the last British units slipped away.

Early in 1919 an Australian historical mission led by C.E.W. Bean (fourth from left) returned to Gallipoli to collect artefacts and assist with research for the official Australian history of the campaign. The group is shown lunching with its Ottoman guide, Major Zeki Bey (second from left). *AWM G01904*

The Allies were justly proud of the highly successful evacuations; the Ottoman peoples could be prouder still of the victory their armies had won. Mustafa Kemal was in İstanbul recuperating from an illness when the Allies evacuated. Some time later, reflecting back on the war, he said:

> [The] English [and Australians] brag about the soldiers and officers who fought gallantly and bravely at Arıburnu landings and at this front. But think about the enemy which landed at Arıburnu shores equipped with the most advanced war machinery and determination, by and large were forced to remain on these shores. Our officers and soldiers who with love for their motherland and religion and heroism protected the doors of their capital İstanbul against such a strong enemy, won the right to a status which we can be proud of. I congratulate all the members of the fighting units under my command. I remember with deep and eternal respect, all the ones who sacrificed their lives and became martyrs for this great objective.[29]

## SIX

# From Atatürk to Anzac Day

The seventh of January 1916 was a day of great celebrations in the small Turkish village near Ankara where the Allied prisoners of war from Gallipoli were being housed. 'Flags flying, bands playing, processions in galore . . .' one Australian prisoner wrote in his diary. 'The explanation given was "The English have been driven off the Dardanelles". We soon found out it was not bluff made in Turkey this time.'[1] Similar celebrations were doubtless occurring across the entire country as news of the victory spread.

In İstanbul, the newspapers of 21 December had carried the news: 'There are no more soldiers in Arı Burnu, and Anafartalar. Our forces are now at the shore and have taken a lot of enemy ammunition, tents, guns, etc.' Over the next few days more details were printed as they became known: 'After their futile attacks to break the heroic Turkish defence the British had to escape taking advantage of heavy fog during the evening.' Finally, on 10 January, an İstanbul paper carried the headline people had waited many months to read: 'The whole Gallipoli peninsula is now free from the enemy. They are driven out of Seddulbahir [sic].'[2]

The Ottoman armies had indeed won a memorable victory by repelling both the navies and the armies of two of Europe's most powerful nations. As self-proclaimed Minister for War, Enver Paşa readily accepted the accolades that come with victory. One such offering was an exquisite, fine silk rug specially woven in his honour. The rug, which measures approximately 1 m × 1.5 m, depicts aerial views of the peninsula battlefield with two insert panels showing several of the forts that successfully guarded the seaway. Woven into the design are the inscriptions:

To the Acting Commander-In-Chief and Minister of War his Excellency
Enver Paşa from the Benevolent Society of Syria this carpet is dedicated
and presented in gratitude in the year 1916.[3]

It is almost certainly not coincidental that a carpet was chosen as the
medium through which to celebrate this great victory. Carpets have
been designed and woven by Turks and others in central Asia and the
Middle East for time immemorial to honour important events and
people. This rug is made of the very finest materials and crafted to the
highest standards imaginable, thereby recording the victory in a
manner that would last virtually for all time. Remarkably, this magnificent rug now resides in Sydney in the collection of esteemed rug
dealer and collector Jacques Cadry. This rug, a unique piece of history
in its own right, is reproduced as the endpages in this book.

Great though it was, the Gallipoli victory did not bring an end
to the bloodshed and destruction encountered by the Ottomans
in the Great War. The alliance with Germany continued, so the
Ottomans were still fighting on several fronts—in Romania and
eastern Anatolia against the Russian armies and in the Middle East
against the British and the Anzacs. After the 1917 Bolshevik Revolution in Russia when Lenin and his comrades created the first
socialist state, Russia (USSR) pulled out of the war. At the front,
Russian and Ottoman troops joined together in peace celebrations
even before the official armistice was declared. Men from opposing
armies shared bread and salt as a symbolic act of peace.

The armistice with the USSR did little, however, to improve
things for the Ottoman armies in the Middle East. These troops, after
some earlier successes, were now fighting a losing war in the deserts.
Their supplies were low and, consequently, morale was poor. Deser-
tion from the ranks was common. In 1917 it was estimated that
300 000 men had deserted; the figure was as large as the regular army
itself! The deserters usually made their way back to Anatolia. Some
formed brigand bands which raided villages and settlements, thereby
adding to the peasants' hardships. Early in 1918, the famous Gallipoli
general, Liman von Sanders and Mustafa Kemal were sent out to
retrieve the situation but their presence made little difference. By the
autumn of 1918, the British and Anzac troops and cavalry units had

captured most of the Middle East or what is now known as Jordan, Syria, Israel, Iraq, Kuwait and Saudi Arabia.

A major aim of the British Middle East campaign had been to capture the region's rich oilfields. Discovery of oil in the Middle East goes back a long way to the days of Babylon when bitumen was used as cement in the walls. In the late nineteenth century, both German and English teams made efforts to locate oil in places such as Iraq, which at that time belonged to the Ottoman Empire. The race to gain control of the oil reserves in the Middle East was won when, in 1918, England occupied the entire Middle East.

The importance of oil had been proven beyond doubt in this war; the Allies were never short of it whereas the Central Powers could not secure adequate supplies. During the war, the number of cars and trucks in the British Army had grown nearly 1000-fold and motorbikes more than 2000-fold. One senior British politician, Lord Curzon, went so far as to say 'the Allies floated to victory on a wave of oil'.[4] In 1925, the newly established Iraqi Petroleum Company gave the rights to the petroleum reserves to England for 75 years. The border between Iraq and Turkey was also drawn to ensure no significant potential petroleum reserves would be accessible to the Turks. Hence, although the 1915 Gallipoli campaign was a failure for the British, within a decade the British Empire had achieved its long-term strategic aim of gaining control of vast reserves of crude oil in the Middle East.

In October 1918, the Young Turks' Union and Progress Government resigned when it became obvious that defeat was imminent. Most of its leaders escaped to Germany. On 30 October 1918, the new government signed an armistice with the Allies. The Ottoman Empire, in decline for several hundred years, had finally crumbled. Enver Paşa fled first to Germany and later tried unsuccessfully to ally himself to the Soviet Union. He then went to Central Asia and organised Turkish/Islamic resistance forces against the Soviet Army. In 1922, Enver Paşa and a handful of his followers were machine gunned by the Red Army near the Pamir Mountains in the Himalayas (where Afghanistan, Pakistan, India, Turkmenistan and China now all have common borders). It was a fitting end for a man who had been instrumental in causing so much death and destruction.

Soldiers crowd into rail trucks near Adana as the Ottoman army demobilises in early 1919. Many men are reputed to have died in accidents or from illness in the terribly cramped conditions. *AWM G02134*

In November 1918, an Allied armada of about fifty ships steamed up the Dardanelles and occupied İstanbul. This time, unlike 1915, not even a single shot was fired against them. The Allied governments had signed an agreement among themselves in 1916 stipulating how the Ottoman Empire would be partitioned after the war. The plan was soon put into action. Early in 1919, French, Italian, British and Greek troops were sent in to occupy much of Anatolia. They encountered very little resistance; the local people were well and truly sick of war. In some places, the occupation forces were actually welcomed because they could reimpose law and order. The British were especially well treated by local officials and in the press.

Mustafa Kemal Paşa, the prominent officer at Gallipoli, was commanding an army in the Middle East when the armistice was declared. He immediately returned to İstanbul and tried to win the position of War Minister in the new government. He was offered instead a position as Inspector-General of remnants of the Ottoman armies in unoccupied north-eastern Anatolia. His task was to bring the area under İstanbul's control. Probably few people suspected that Mustafa Kemal would become the leader of a national liberation struggle.

Mustafa Kemal moved to Anatolia and unified the forces against the occupation armies. He succeeded in bringing together widely diverse groups: professional army staff whose prestige and future prospects were poor; Muslim landlords and the merchants of eastern and central Anatolia who expected to lose financially from the occupation; and the intelligentsia who supported the cause of nationalism. The mass of peasants understandably were not eager to embark upon another war. They were soon convinced otherwise, however, when the occupying forces proved much less friendly than had been anticipated. The concept of the holy war against the invading infidel was again used to mobilise the people. On 23 April 1920, this new coalition formed a Grand National Assembly in Ankara. The Assembly resolved to drive the occupying infidel forces from the country and release the sultan from their control. In reality it was just as much an insurrection against the sultan and the Ankara government later abolished the puppet Imperial Court.

Meanwhile, the surviving remnants of the Ottoman armies in Anatolia were reorganised and strengthened. A treaty was signed with the Soviets early in 1921 which secured the eastern border. In the west, in 1919, Greek armies supported and backed by Britain began the invasion of Turkey at İzmir and had advanced almost to Ankara by 1921. They were finally checked at the Battle of Sakarya which lasted twenty-two days. This proved the turning point, but it took Mustafa Kemal and his forces another year to push the Greek armies out of Anatolia. The French and Italians had, in the meantime, signed pacts with the Turks and withdrawn their forces. The British forces finally left İstanbul and Çanakkale late in 1922. The sultan went with them. During 1923, as part of the peace treaty, over a million Greeks in Anatolia and about half a million Turks in the Balkans were forcibly uprooted and exchanged between the countries. This no doubt caused great heartbreak to those leaving their homelands.

Through these various means, the people of Anatolia, under the brilliant leadership of Mustafa Kemal, had by 1923 driven out all occupying forces, against strong odds. After the final victory was secured, Mustafa Kemal engineered the formation of a secular republic with a parliament based on the French model of government. It was a notable feat in a country so committed to Islam. Mustafa Kemal was elected Turkey's first president on 29 October 1923.

The country desperately needed time to rebuild. It had weathered nearly fifteen years of continuous war. The ranks of its menfolk had been decimated, many villages were deserted, and much valuable land lay fallow. It would take even longer to heal people's physical and emotional wounds. Kemal and his government instituted a series of reforms aimed at breaking ties with the Ottoman past and shaping a new society along Western lines. Religious schools and courts were abolished (1924); secular family law was adopted and wearing of *fez* prohibited (1925); the Western calendar and Greenwich time were adopted, and new banknotes and coins put into circulation (1925); the Latin alphabet replaced Arabic script (1928); and surnames were made compulsory for the first time. Many non-Turkish words were outlawed and replaced by suitable Turkish equivalents. Women won the right to vote and stand for parliament in 1934. In practically every facet of life, Turkish nationalism became the state ideology. In 1934, Mustafa Kemal was given the surname Atatürk—father of the Turks.

Reconstruction activities gathered pace over subsequent years. The economic system was reformed and various state enterprises took on major developmental projects. Gradually, the railways, schools, hospitals, factories and other institutions were improved and augmented. The program was not without its victims. Internal opposition was not tolerated and any resistance was forcibly put down. Religious and Kurdish revolts, for example, were suppressed vigorously. Mustafa Kemal died on 10 November 1938. He is still so deeply revered by Turks today that his photo hangs in all public buildings and in many private homes.

### '. . . your sons and daughters have become our sons and daughters'

Despite the many reforms to Turkish society and economy, life remained hard for the village peasants, even though Mustafa Kemal once declared that 'the peasants are the masters of our country'. Come the mid-1950s, they were the ones who migrated to urban areas and later went overseas in search of jobs.

'If you have no ammunition you have your bayonets.'
This rug, produced in the İsparta region of western
Turkey in the 1930s, illustrates the pivotal role that
Gallipoli played in creating Mustafa Kemal's image as
the saviour and maker of modern Turkey. *Kindly lent
by Jacques Cadry*

During the first quarter of this century, most parts of Anatolia
underwent dramatic economic transformation and experienced a
prolonged economic recession. Furthermore, the demographic com-
position of Turkey was completely shaken by years of war. Turkey
did not actively participate in World War II until 1945, when it
entered on the side of the Allies. Nevertheless, the economic recession which accompanied the War further hampered the population

growth. It was not until the late 1940s that the secondary effects of the 'missing' age groups diminished and new health programs reduced the incidence of plague and other chronic diseases. Turkey then experienced a phenomenon common to many underdeveloped countries: population growth outstripping economic growth.

Unable to cope with the pressures of a population explosion, a painfully slow rate of industrialisation and an ever-growing balance of payments deficit, the Turkish Government sought relief by encouraging people to emigrate. In so doing, the Turks were following the example set after World War II by other Mediterranean countries. Greece, Italy and other such countries had established migration programs with developed countries like Germany and Australia to help solve their own economic difficulties. Australia was eager to accept migrants to work in its factories.

On 5 October 1967, Australia signed an agreement with Turkey whereby the Australian Government would meet the transportation and reception costs of bringing Turkish migrants to Australia. Turkey was the first developing country with which Australia signed an assisted migration agreement. According to an Australian researcher studying Turkish migrants, Joy Elley, the Australians embarked on the project only after a prolonged debate and the redefinition of Turkey as a European rather than a Middle Eastern country.[5] Soon, Turks began arriving in sizeable numbers as the flow of migrants from Australia's more traditional sources diminished. Turkish migration also heralded the end of the White Australia policy.

Prior to the introduction of this scheme, very few Turkish people lived in Australia. The 1966 census, for example, set the figure at less than 3000, most of whom were Turkish Cypriots. In the ten months from October 1968 to July 1969, fifty-eight charter flights of Turkish migrants arrived in Australia. Most of the passengers disembarked and settled in Melbourne and Sydney. By the mid-1970s, the net migration of Turkish people to Australia totalled about 14 000 people.

Australia was not the only country to which Turks migrated in this period. In fact, many more Turks moved to other parts of Europe, particularly Germany, than came to Australia. Between 1961 and 1980, for example, the Turkish Government Employment Service provided 916 000 placements for Turkish workers overseas.

Excitement runs high after Qantas flight QF174.027 lands at Sydney Airport on 14 October 1968 carrying 168 Turkish passengers, the first group of government assisted migrants to come from Turkey. *Commonwealth Department of Immigration 68/4/22*

Of these, 72 per cent went to Germany, while only a fraction migrated to Australia.[6] It was not long before these migration programs became a commonly accepted alternative to working in Turkey. By the mid-1970s, there were over 1.5 million Turkish migrants dispersed across more than thirty countries.

Most of the Turks who came to Australia in the late 1960s and early 1970s were unskilled labourers and peasants with little or no knowledge of English. The unskilled component was, in fact, higher than that of most other ethnic groups coming to Australia at that time. The flow of Turkish migrants to Australia did not follow the European pattern. The Australian Government sought permanent settlers whereas Germany, for example, demanded that all expatriate workers under the 'guest worker program' return to Turkey when their contracts expired. Most Turks migrated to Australia as families, unlike migration to Germany where the husband usually went alone and left his family back in Turkey. Compared to Germany, the number of Turks migrating to Australia was very small.

Faced by a severe economic recession in the late 1970s, the Australian Government cut back its assisted migration scheme considerably. It also reduced its family reunion and sponsored migration program. From the early 1980s onwards, permanent visas were given only to the highly skilled, thus the number of Turkish arrivals substantially decreased. At the beginning of the twenty-first century, it is very difficult for Turks, like other non-English speaking applicants, to obtain visas for permanent residence in Australia, even under the family reunion and humanitarian categories. According to the 2001 Census 53 000 Australians describe themselves as being of Turkish ancestry.[7]

Why might a Turk consider coming to Australia? Poor economic prospects back in Turkey are the most often stated reason. Many also came seeking a better education for their children. The majority of the early arrivals intended to stay only for a short while, rather like the European guest worker schemes. Soon, however, chain migration started among relatives and fellow villagers. Today, most of these early migrants seem happy to stay in Australia. This probably reflects a realisation that the political climate in Turkey remains unstable and the economic outlook has not substantially improved over time. Also, those workers who came to Australia to work and save for two years are now very accustomed to life in Australia; certainly their children are. Some of the pioneer migrants subsequently returned to Turkey 'for good', only to return to Australia. On the other hand, most migrants with professional qualifications who arrived from Turkey after 1980 came to Australia with no intention of returning to their birthplace. One way or another, it seems migration generally proves to be a one-way ticket.

In *The Turks in Australia*, a book specially produced to mark the twenty-fifth anniversary of large-scale migration from Turkey to Australia, the then prime ministers of both countries wrote forewords reflecting on this milestone. Each congratulated the migrants on the contributions they were making to Australia's development and multicultural society. Significantly, each leader also acknowledged that the foundations for this mutual respect were laid at

Gallipoli. Echoing Atatürk's famous words, Australian prime minister Paul Keating expressed his delight 'that your sons and daughters have become our sons and daughters'.[8]

Today, Australia's Turkish migrants live in the same streets, work in the same factories and offices and attend the same schools as other Australians. And, of course, they enjoy the same public holidays as the rest of the community, including Anzac Day.

What do Turkish migrants feel on Anzac Day? What do they think about the Australian involvement in the Çanakkale war? How do Turkish children react to the topic as it is taught in the classroom at a typical Australian school?

Many of the early Turkish migrants learned only after coming to Australia that Australians fought at Çanakkale. They report that although the battles were taught at school in Turkey, generally, Australia was not mentioned. A large proportion of Turkish migrants, particularly those who arrived in the first two decades of the migration scheme, had had only a short period of formal schooling in Turkey, so it is not surprising that they knew little about Australia. However, until comparatively recently, even the better educated often did not associate the word Anzac with either Australia or New Zealand. As one Turkish migrant commented: 'In history books at school Anzacs were mentioned but you usually wondered who these people might be. If you were careful enough, you would note that Anzacs were soldiers from British colonies.'[9] Knowledge of the Australian and New Zealand involvement at Çanakkale was generally limited to well-educated migrants, or the descendants of war veterans, or those who had a family member in the armed services. However, as was described in chapter one, the strong interest shown by Australians and New Zealanders over the past decade or so in attending the Anzac Day Dawn Ceremony at Anzac Cove has helped to substantially improve Turkish people's general awareness of the Gallipoli campaign.

Once in Australia, most Turks learned about Australia's Çanakkale either in school or at work. How did they respond to this revelation? 'I did not feel angry when I learned that Australians were among the enemy in Çanakkale. It was long, long ago', reflected Mustafa Yıldırım, an 88-year-old Turkish migrant who served at

Çanakkale in 1915, when he was interviewed in Melbourne in the early 1980s.[10] A Turkish woman recalls her office friends asking if she felt embarrassed as Anzac Day approached. She told them, 'If there was anyone to be embarrassed, it certainly isn't me. My country was fighting for her independence and we defeated the invaders.'[11] Another migrant remembers that he '. . . felt silly standing up for Australian soldiers' at his school Anzac Day service back in 1970. He adds, 'I ended up discussing it more physically than verbally during recess . . . The Australian kids got jealous that Turks won the war.'[12] Thankfully, things are now very different. Whether their origins be Australian or Turkish, today's students are likely to regard Gallipoli as part of their common heritage. We asked some Turkish–Australians if the fact that Australians fought at Çanakkale has any influence on what they think about or feel for Australians. Practically every respondent emphatically replied in words to the effect, 'No . . . Why should it?' As one Turkish-born woman who has lived in Australia since 1974 put it: 'On Anzac Day [2002], I did not feel anything. We now belong here. Australians do not harm us. Our children are married here. We are not likely to go back to Turkey.'[13] A 50-year-old woman who has lived in Australia for thirty years, having migrated in 1972, offered this more pensive reply:

> On Anzac Day [2002] I felt very sad. It was painful to be a worker in a country which had attacked us. I cried a lot wondering why we had to come and work here. They [Australians] lost many soldiers which they are remembering on Anzac Day. But recently friendship began after the Turks migrated here. The new generation is trying to do something. It is not nice to continue being enemies, but what is the depth of friendship, that I do not know.[14]

Several of our respondents gave answers which showed their respect for Australia's traditions and lifestyle but questioned why this country should ever have become involved in such a distant war. Thus, a 26-year-old Australian woman of Turkish ancestry commented:

> It does not worry me that Australians fought at Gallipoli because it was a long time ago. Australia is a free country. We live in peace. I am teaching my children all things Australian: Christmas, Easter, Anzac Day. On Anzac Day, not to offend our neighbours, we don't mow the lawn and treat

the day with respect. But I still can't understand how England asked Australians to join in a war against Turkey. It seems utterly absurd. However, that was a long time ago. I feel deeply on Anzac Day. My [paternal] grandfather had fought at Gallipoli with Atatürk; he has many medals and had lost his hearing due to bombs exploding near him.[15]

A 69-year-old man resident in Australia for 30 years similarly remarked:

> Australians came all the way to Turkey and lost the war. We should celebrate on Anzac Day, not them [Australians]. We like Australians and respect them. We are angry with the ones [British] who brought them to Turkey. These people [Australians] are good people, they looked after us well, gave us jobs or unemployment benefits.[16]

Turks understand only too well the devastating effects wars can have on the individual, the society, the economy and the environment. Almost every Turkish adult now living in Australia would personally know someone directly affected by some or all the misfortunes war and post-war conditions can bring. Thus, the Australians have the full sympathy of most Turks. As one middle-aged Turkish-born woman lamented:

> I get sad on Anzac Day for the ones who died. A lot of blood flowed for no reason. The ones who died also had mothers and fathers. I feel for both sides. I feel sad for the present wars as well. It takes many years of hard work to raise a child. Nobody likes or wants them to die.[17]

The observations of one Turkish woman seem to say it all:

> The Anzac Day march was just like any similar national day in Turkey. I was shattered to see the war veterans in their uniforms and medals marching down with their grandchildren. Were these people, marching down with an expression so similar to what our war veterans would have on their faces, the ENEMY? Then my mind was battered with the questions: why should there be wars? Why should people ever be put in a position of being enemies?[18]

It takes two sides to fight a war and, invariably the soldiers (and often the civilians) of both countries suffer regardless of who 'wins'.

## The painful memory

The futility and personal tragedy of Gallipoli (and war in general) is conveyed with immense poignancy in the epic poem, *Human landscapes from my country*, written in the early 1940s by Turkey's most famous poet, Nazım Hikmet. Hikmet was jailed for many years and his poems were banned by the Turkish authorities because of his political beliefs and strong commitment to peace. In 1950 he was awarded the World Peace Prize. Nazım Hikmet died in 1963.

However, recently the Turkish authorities began to recognise the international appeal of Turkey's famous poet and began to embrace his works and memory. In fact, on the occasion of the hundredth anniversary of his birth, UNESCO declared 2002 to be the year of Nazım Hikmet, recognition which is supported and even celebrated by several government and community organised events.

*Human landscapes from my country* is a poetic saga of more than 17 000 lines. Part of the saga are the words of a Turkish Çanakkale veteran reminiscing to a group of passengers in the corridor of a train. He tells them how he received eight wounds at the great Ottoman counter-offensive of 19 May and the terrible pain he subsequently endured. Hikmet's message is universal, and in that is the danger and the hope for us all.

> . . . I was wounded in eight places on
> The night of 6 May[19]
> We were fighting the English,[20]
> Their trenches so close
> Their grenades reaching our trenches
> And ours theirs.
> We rose to attack
> I was hit before taking three steps . . .
> After a while,
> I lifted my head and looked up:
> Stars in the sky.
> Our unit had moved back.
> Trenches of English firing continuously.[21]
> Bullets passing
> Over my head.
> I started to crawl back . . .

The fallen martyrs touch me,
Actually I am touching them . . .
Some with blood in their open mouths,
Some face down,
Some on their knees,
Some with guns in their hands . . .
I prayed to Allah
'If you are going to kill me
It should be so,
With a gun in my hand . . .
Facing the infidel . . .'
It was morning when . . .
I managed to get to our trenches . . .
Twenty-five metres
In three hours.
I stayed curled up in the trench for a while . . .
My wounds started hurting.
Around noon they put me on the back of a mate.
I was taken back to the division.
Tents . . .
Straw strewn between the tent poles.
Wounded of many kinds laying on the straw.
Some crying
Some swearing.
They cut my uniform off
Left me as naked as I was born,
And later put a cloak over me.
No bandages.
Wounds open.
But, thanks to Allah
No bleeding, the wounds being
Mixed with earth and dried up . . .
By the time the sun was setting
They took us out . . .
Medics put us on horsecarts.
One on top of another,
Like empty wheat bags . . .
Ten, fifteen wounded on a cart.
Some cry out
Some die that minute . . .
The roads of Arı Burnu are bumpy.
It is dark.
I am lying on my back.

Another body underneath wriggles,
On my chest, a pair of legs, but
Half of one is missing.
We are going downhill.
The sky full of stars.
Light wind blowing . . .
By morning we arrived at the pier.
There is a tent.
Someone shouts from inside the tent:
'Where are you from?'
'Such and such.'
'What is your father's name?'
'So and so.'
'What is your name?'
'So and so.'
'Driver throw him down.'
The pain is unbearable.
I swore at the driver.
Obviously used to this, he said
'Swear my brother,
As much as you like.'
We were laid on the sand.
The sea comes and goes . . .
Maybe a thousand wounded on the beach,
Maybe more.
In the afternoon
Came a ship:
With two stacks,
Painted the colour of the sea
They loaded us on to it
Shouting, swearing
Again like empty bags.
Inside the ship it was hell.
Blood squelching,
Steam,
Oil,
Sweat.
They took me down to the hold.
We sailed.
Seven days seven nights.
Maggots appeared in my wounds . . .
Black headed
White bodied . . .

Maggots are smart,
When I look, they bury
Themselves in the wounds.
Seven days seven nights.
If Allah doesn't kill, he doesn't.
The Turk is strong,
He can endure . . .
Around nightfall, I was taken ashore . . .
İstanbul glittering.
My precious İstanbul.
We entered a hospital.
The walls gleaming white . . .
They put me on a trolley.
So comfortable.
May Allah save the state.
I prayed for the state then . . .'


. . . A student
(Who was listening to the story) . . .
Thought to himself: . . .
'Am I brave enough
To await death in a trench?
The ones who did and even died
Were they brave? . . .
Does this usually have anything
To do with being brave?
Or are the ones in the trenches
Sheep and cattle
Being led to their slaughter by a network of shepherds
Captured not only by their bodies
But also by their minds? . . .'[22]

# Postscript: Symbols for tomorrow?

Now that the last Gallipoli veteran has passed away, we have no living links with the 1915 battles. What does remain, of course, is the land itself: the narrow beaches, the craggy cliffs and gently sloping plains on which nearly a million men fought, lived and, in many cases, died. Recognising the sanctity of this ground, in 1973 the Turkish government designated 33 000 hectares (330 square kilometres) of land at the southern tip of the peninsula as the Gallipoli Peninsula National Historical Park. Expanding on this initiative and following the 1994 bushfires, in 1997 the government convened an international competition to re-evaluate, restore and rehabilitate the area as a park dedicated to peace. The competition was organised under the auspices of the International Union of Architects, with a nine-member judging panel, including Australia's Glenn Murcutt, New Zealand's Tony Watkins along with architects from seven other countries, and managed by Ankara's METU University. The Peace Park Competition looks 'to the new millennium for inspiration and aims to create a setting where alternatives to war can be imagined and encouraged'.[1]

Undoubtedly, the land itself will continue to be seen as sacred soil by Turks, Australians and New Zealanders for generations to come. But gradually the land is reverting to its natural state; all the scars inflicted on it in 1915 are slowly disappearing. It is thus worth reflecting for a moment on what else might become the enduring symbols of the Çanakkale battles, especially what things might become the key material icons for Australia, New Zealand and Turkey.

A few days after Anzac Day 2002, an Echuca (Victoria) man

went to his local police station and handed in a velvet-lined box containing a mummified skull with two bullet holes through it. He claimed it was the remains of a Turkish soldier from Gallipoli, brought back to Australia at the end of the war by an Anzac, his grandfather. He and his family, the newspapers asserted, now feel 'too embarrassed' to keep the gruesome souvenir any longer.[2] His family were not the only ones embarrassed by the macabre 'trophy'. Neither the Australian nor Turkish governments seemed comfortable in their responses to the incident. How could anyone prove if the skull was indeed a Gallipoli souvenir? Even if it could be shown to be of approximately the right age, its ethnic origin would seem impossible to determine. So should the story be accepted at face value or dismissed as a tasteless hoax? Should the head be given to a museum, given a dignified burial in Australia, or returned to Turkey? After considerable reflection, the two governments decided that although they could not definitively link the head to Gallipoli, the diplomatic thing to do was bury it on the Gallipoli peninsula. As a consequence, hopefully Gallipoli's last prize will finally find peace.

In many respects, the really interesting thing about this grisly tale is not whether the head was actually an Australian soldier's ghoulish souvenir, but the universal embarrassment that greeted news of its unearthing. The family clearly felt embarrassed to be in possession of it; similarly, every level of officialdom in both Australia and Turkey that was drawn into the debate made their discomfort plain to see. It is questionable if the same sense of embarrassment would have been shared by earlier generations of Australians. For some of our forebears, war trophies (authentic or otherwise) were treasured as highly as their campaign medals. Viewed against this background, perhaps the story actually provides a positive message: namely, that Australian and Turkish people now share a desire to build close links founded on the mutual respect born at Gallipoli and incidents such as the mysterious mummified head will not deflect people from this goal.

Far less grotesque, but potentially even more controversial, is the future fate of the Australian submarine *AE2*. As was described on page 89, this 53.65-metre-long vessel carried the first Australians into the Gallipoli campaign when it slipped through the Narrows hours before any troops stormed the beaches. *AE2* will always hold a place of distinction in the campaign as the first Allied naval vessel to penetrate the Turkish defences and reach the Sea of Marmara. News of its success encouraged the Allied land forces commander, General Sir Ian Hamilton, to reject requests to evacuate the Anzac troops hours after their initial landings. But the submarine's glory was short-lived—after five days of creating havoc among the Ottoman Navy and its supply lines, *AE2* was scuttled by its captain after it had been disabled by the Turkish torpedo boat *Sultanhisar*.

On 2 July 1998, Selçuk Kolay, the Director of the Rahmi M Koç Museum in İstanbul, located the wreck of the *AE2* in 73 metres of water four nautical miles north-north-west of Karaburun Point in the Sea of Marmara. An accomplished scuba diver, Kolay had spent four years searching for the wreck. A small Australian dive team, supported by the Royal Australian Navy, had worked with Kolay in 1997. They returned in October 1998 to assist in reconnoitring the newly discovered wreck site. It is a difficult site to visit; the extreme depth requires divers to use special mixed gases apparatus and their bottom time is restricted to twelve minutes or less.

According to one of the Australian divers, 'as a proverbial "time capsule" [*AE2*] . . . is quite unique'.[3] Its crew sank it by flooding its valves and leaving open the conning tower hatch as they abandoned ship; the Turkish torpedo boat had inflicted only minimal damage. Ironically, Turkish fishing nets have caused more damage over the decades fouling the vessel's superstructure than did the initial naval attack. The 800-ton hull now sits upright on the seafloor, showing only limited signs of corrosion on its outer plating. Thus, *AE2* survives as Gallipoli's largest intact war relic.

Now that it's been rediscovered, what should be done? Could it, should it be raised, or is it best to leave it where it rests? Equally importantly, who owns it: Turkey or Australia? If there were any war dead still aboard, these questions would need no answers as international naval convention dictates that war grave sites must not be disturbed. But all *AE2*'s crew left the boat safely, thus over-coming this potential hurdle. Some maritime archaeologists tend to favour leaving wrecks where they find them, employing non-disturbance archaeological techniques to map and photograph the site. Using Internet technology, they point out, virtual visitors around the world could inspect the wreck from their own living rooms.

Yet most archaeologists agree that not every shipwreck must be left untouched. Sometimes, unique technical design or construction details require the wreck be raised for examination. Some wrecks hold historically valuable materials that justify their raising. Arguably, *AE2* meets both criteria. It is the most complete example of its type known and houses a veritable treasure trove of personal effects documenting life on board. 'Information on victualling, stowage, living conditions, social stratification in terms of duties and functions, hardships and danger can all be expected to be obtained', according to an Australian maritime archaeologist who has dived on the site.[4]

Most experts agree that, while difficult, it is technically feasible to salvage and conserve the hull for public display. Similarly, employing the full suite of modern conservation techniques could save and preserve many of the written records and personal effects still entombed aboard. Of course, all this could be very expensive and would undoubtedly take many years to complete.

But this should not be seen as a deterrent; the conservation process would become a major attraction, especially if it were located near to the battle zone, ideally at Çanakkale. The idea has already been mooted in both Turkey and Australia, most notably by former Australian Defence Minister and Federal Opposition Leader, Kim Beazley, when he spoke during Parliament's condolence motion for Alec Campbell:

> In conclusion might I say that our commemoration of the battlefield is not yet complete. I recommend that the government start the process of taking up the Australian submarine, *AE2*, which has been found by the Turks. I hope that by the time of the centenary of Gallipoli in 2015 there will be an appropriate interpretation centre there, too, for it. Fortunately or unfortunately, the submarine's success in penetrating the Dardanelles is what caused the Australians to hang onto the beaches. I commend the government for undertaking a joint consideration and I hope it comes to a successful conclusion.[5]

There is no doubt that *AE2* could become an important symbol for Australians and Turks alike. Its recovery and conservation would become a focal point for both countries' remembrance, cooperation and friendship. The future is very likely to unfold interesting new pages in the Gallipoli saga.

# *Notes*

## Introduction
1 Melbourne *Age,* 18 May 2002.
2 *Sydney Morning Herald*, 25 May 2002.
3 ibid., 17 May 2002.

## Chapter One—A special bond
1 H. Kannengiesser, quoted in North, p. 21.
2 Melbourne *Age*, 22 September 1983.
3 Melbourne *Age*, 18 August 1983.
4 Bracks, speech notes, 21 July 2002.
5 Priest, speech notes, 6 June 2002.
6 *The Australian,* 25 April 2000.
7 Bastiaan, p. 2, Melbourne *Age*, 19 March 1985.
8 Tunçoku, p. 194.
9 ibid., p. 20.
10 ibid., p. 23.
11 *Cumhuriyet* newspaper, 16 May 1999.
12 ibid., 18 May 2000.
13 ibid., 16 March 2001.
14 ibid., 5 June 2002.
15 Başarın, *The Turks in Australia*, p. 66.
16 *AM* radio program, Australian Broadcasting Commission, 17 May 2002.
17 Priest, speech notes, 6 June 2002.
18 Carlyon, 'The influence of the Gallipoli campaigns on Australia and Turkey', Union of Australian Friends of Turkey (Victorian Branch) *Newsletter*, p. 9.
19 Students' travel diary, Upfield Secondary College (Victoria) 1998.
20 Official invitation.
21 Roland, p. 58.

22  Melbourne *Age,* 22 January 2000.
23  Banoğlu, p. 114.
24  Scates, p. 13.

**Chapter Two—A proud heritage**
1  Sampson, p. 72.
2  Gammage, p. 7.
3  Firth, p. 130.
4  Kennedy, p. 130.

**Chapter Three—Defending the homeland**
1  Aspinall-Oglander, vol. 1, p. 33.
2  ibid., p. 35.
3  Puleston, p. 39.
4  Muhlmann, pp. 71–2.
5  Keyes, p. 260.
6  Kannengiesser, p. 134.
7  ibid., p. 136.
8  Bean, *Gallipoli Mission*, p. 278.
9  North, p. 357.
10  Muhlmann, p. 85.
11  Gillam, pp. 5–6.
12  Murray J., p. 53.
13  ibid., p. 61.
14  Muhlmann, p. 91.
15  Bean, *Official History*, vol. 1, p. 250.
16  Melbourne *Age*, *Good Weekend*, 18 April 1986.
17  Melbourne *Herald*, 9 February 1990.
18  von Sanders, p. 63.
19  Eşref, p. 17.
20  Bean, *Gallipoli Mission*, pp. 131–3.
21  Callwell, p. 96.
22  Air Commodore Samson, quoted in Moorehead, p. 100.
23  Creighton, p. 62.
24  ibid., p. 59.
25  ibid., p. 62.
26  ibid., p. 60.
27  Puleston, p. 80.
28  Liddle, p. 111.
29  Murray J., pp. 68–9.
30  von Sanders, pp. 70–1.
31  Keyes, p. 302.

32  Denham, p. 96.
33  Bean, *Official History*, vol. 1, p. 505.
34  Kemal, pp. 10–11.
35  Bean, *Official History*, vol. 1, p. 514.
36  Gammage, p. 65.

**Chapter Four—'. . . a brave and tenacious enemy'**
1  Gammage, p. 59.
2  ibid., p. 91.
3  ibid., p. 90.
4  Dawnay, 19 June 1915.
5  Murray J., p. 75.
6  Creighton, p 100.
7  Ashmead-Bartlett, *Despatches*, p. 83.
8  Liddle, p. 115.
9  Bean, *Gallipoli Mission*, p. 357.
10  Bean, *Official History*, vol. 2, pp. 139–40.
11  ibid., p. 140.
12  Hanman, p. 123.
13  Bean, *Official History*, vol. 2, p. 155.
14  ibid., p. 161.
15  ibid.
16  Fewster, p. 106.
17  Bean, *Gallipoli Mission*, p. 358.
18  Bean, *Official History*, vol. 2, p. 162.
19  De Loghe, p. 235.
20  ibid., p. 250.
21  Beeston, p. 30.
22  Gammage, p. 105.
23  Liddle, p. 154.
24  North, p. 209.
25  Bean, *Gallipoli Mission*, p. 59.
26  Gammage, p. 92.
27  Bean, *Official History*, vol. 2, p. 206.
28  Muhlmann, p. 155.
29  Brown, pp. 14–15.
30  Lushington, p. 18.
31  Wheat, p. 22.
32  ibid., pp. 21–2.
33  ibid.
34  Banoğlu, p. 56.

35  Murray J., p. 95.
36  Kannengiesser, p. 163.
37  Gammage, p. 77.
38  Kannengiesser, p. 120.
39  von Sanders, p. 75.
40  Kannengiesser, p. 140.
41  ibid., pp. 122–3.
42  ibid., p. 122.
43  ibid., p. 125.
44  ibid.
45  ibid., p. 133.
46  ibid., p. 163.
47  ibid.
48  ibid., p. 132.
49  Interview with Mustafa Yıldırım.
50  Eşref, p. 35.

**Chapter Five—Honour is restored**
1  von Sanders, p. 82.
2  Sampson, p. 72.
3  Moorehead, p. 164.
4  Bean, *Gallipoli Mission*, pp. 184–5.
5  ibid., p. 193.
6  ibid., p. 198.
7  Gammage, p. 71.
8  East, p. 69.
9  Gammage, pp. 71–2.
10  Bean, *Official History*, vol. 2, p. 564.
11  Kemal, p. 31.
12  Gammage, p. 75.
13  Laffin, p. 133.
14  Kemal, pp. 34–5.
15  Orga, p. 85.
16  Kemal, p. 42.
17  Eşref, p. 39.
18  Bean, *Gallipoli Mission*, p. 223.
19  Orga, p. 89.
20  Bean, *Official History*, vol. 2, p. 714.
21  Gammage, p. 93.
22  ibid., pp. 92–3.
23  ibid., pp. 93–4.

24  ibid., p. 93.
25  *Anzac Book*, p. 165.
26  ibid., pp. 58–9.
27  Bean, *Gallipoli Mission*, p. 251.
28  Ibid., p. 252.
29  Eşref, p. 37.

**Chapter Six—From Atatürk to Anzac Day**

1  Wheat, pp. 28–9.
2  Banoğlu, pp. 65, 68.
3  Johnson, p. 32.
4  Tugendhat, p. 71.
5  Elley, p. 50.
6  TC Çalışma Bakanlığı, p. 21.
7  Australian Bureau of Statistics, 2001.
8  Başarın, *The Turks in Australia*, p. ix.
9  Interview with authors, 1984.
10  ibid.
11  ibid.
12  ibid.
13  ibid.
14  ibid.
15  ibid.
16  ibid.
17  ibid.
18  ibid., 1984.
19  According to the Islamic calendar. The poem describes the events of 19 May 1915 according to the western calendar.
20  The Ottomans often referred to the Anzacs as 'the English'.
21  See previous note.
22  Hikmet, pp. 72–8, translated by V. Başarın.

**Postscript: Symbols for tomorrow?**

1  Turkish Ministry of Forestry, *The Gallipoli Peace Park International . . . Competition.*
2  *The Australian*, 2 May 2002.
3  Smith, p. 14.
4  ibid., p. 17.
5  *Hansard*, House of Representatives, 17 June 2002, p. 2997.

# Bibliography

Abadan Unat, N., 'Dış göç akımının Türk kadınının "özgürleşme" ve "sözde özgürleşme" sürecine etkisi', *Amme İdaresi Dergisi*, vol. 10, no. 1, 1977.

Abadan Unat, N., et al., 'Turkish Migration to Europe, 1960–1975', *Turkish Workers in Europe 1960–1975* (London, 1976).

Akdağ, M., *Türk Halkının Dirlik ve Düzenlik Kavgası* (Ankara, 1975).

Alşar, E., *Türkiye Cumhuriyeti Tarihi* (İstanbul, 1981).

*Anzac Book* (London, 1916).

Ashmead-Bartlett, E., *Despatches from the Dardanelles* (London, 1915).

Aspinall-Oglander, C.F., *History of the Great War Gallipoli*, vols. 1 and 2 (London, 1929, 1932).

Australian Bureau of Statistics, *2001 Census of Population and Housing* (Canberra, 2002).

Avcıoğlu, D., *Milli Kurtuluş Tarihi* (İstanbul, 1974).

Aybars, E., *İstiklal Mahkemeleri* (Ankara, 1975).

Aydemir, S.S., *Enver Paşa: Makedonyadan Orta Asyaya*, vols. 1, 2 and 3 (İstanbul, 1972).

——*Tek Adam Mustafa Kemal*, vols. 1, 2, 3 (İstanbul, 1976).

——*İkinci Adam* (İstanbul, 1976).

——*Suyu Arayan Adam* (İstanbul, 1976).

Aytur, M., *Kalkınma Yarışı ve Türkiye* (Ankara, 1970).

Banoğlu, N.A., *Türk Basınında Çanakkale Günleri* (İstanbul, 1982).

Başarın, H.H. & Başarın, V. *The Turks in Australia* (Melbourne, 1993).

Bastiaan, R., *Gallipoli Plaques* (Melbourne, 1990).

Bracks, S., *Speech Notes*, Melbourne, 21 July 2001.

Bean, C.E.W., *Gallipoli Mission* (Canberra, 1952).

——*The Official History of Australia in the War of 1914–1918*, vols. 1 and 2 (Sydney, 1921, 1924).

Beeston, J.L., *Five Months at Anzac* (Sydney, 1916).

Billett, R.S., *War Trophies* (Sydney, 1999).

Blair, J.M., *The Control of Oil* (New York, 1978).

Brenchley, F & E., *Stoker's Submarine* (Sydney, 2001).

Brown, H.A., 'Personal Diary' (Mitchell Library, Sydney, MSS 5 7–594C).

Callwell, C.E., *The Dardanelles* (London, 1919).

Carlyon, L., *Gallipoli* (Sydney, 2001).

Cassar, G.H., *The French and the Dardanelles* (London, 1971).

Clark, C.M.H., *A History of Australia*, vol. 5, 1888–1915 (Melbourne, 1981).

Commonwealth of Australia Department of Immigration, 'Survey of Turkish Workers' (Canberra, 1971).

Creighton, Rev. O., *With the Twenty-Ninth Division: A Chaplain's Experience* (London, 1916).

Dawnay, G., Personal Papers (Imperial War Museum, London).

De Loghe, S., *The Straits Impregnable* (London, 1917).

Denham, H.M., *Dardanelles: A Midshipman's Diary* (London, 1981).

Dyer, M.G., 'The End of World War I in Turkey, 1918–1919' (PhD thesis, London University, 1972).

East, R. (ed), *The Gallipoli Diary of Sargeant Lawrence* (Carlton, 1981).

Elley, J., 'The Maintenance of Turkish Identity in the Migration Situation', R. Akçelik (ed.), *Change and Persistence of Turkish Culture* (Melbourne, 1984).

Eşref, R., *Mustafa Kemal Çanakkale'yi Anlatıyor* (Ankara, 1981).

Fewster, K., *Gallipoli Correspondent. The Frontline Diary of C.E.W. Bean* (Sydney, 1983).

Firth, S.G., 'Social Values in the New South Wales Primary School 1880–1914: An Analysis of School Texts', *Melbourne Studies in Education, 1970* (Melbourne, 1970).

Frame, T.R. & Swinden, G.J., *First in, Last out. The Navy at Gallipoli* (Kenthurst, 1990).

Gammage, B., *The Broken Years* (Canberra, 1974).

Gençcan, M.I., *Çanakkale Savaşlarında Altın Harfler* (1992).

Gillam, J.G., *Gallipoli Diary* (London, 1918).

Gunesen, F. *Çanakkale Savaşları* (İstanbul, 1986).

Hanman, E.F., *Twelve Months with the 'Anzacs'* (Brisbane, 1916).

*Harp Mecmuası*. No. 3 (İstanbul, 1915).

Hikmet, N., *Memleketimden İnsan Manzaraları* (Ankara, n.d.).

Ilgar, İ., *Çanakkale Savaşları 1915* (Ankara, 1982).

İnalcık, H., *The Ottoman Empire: The Classical Age 1300–1600* (London, 1973).

Johnson, P. (ed), *Woven History. Stories in Carpets* (Sydney, 1990).

Kannengiesser, H., *Gallipoli; Bedeutung and Verlauf der Kempe, 1915* (Berlin, 1927).

Karatay, B.V., *Mehmetçik ve Anzaklar* (Ankara, 1987).

Kaylan, A., *Çanakkale İçinde Vurdular Beni* (İstanbul, n.d.).

Kemal, M., *Atatürk's Memoirs of the Anafartalar Battles* (London, n.d.).

Kennedy, B., *Silver, Sin and Sixpenny Ale. A Social History of Broken Hill, 1883–1921* (Melbourne, 1978).

Kerr, G., *Lost Anzacs* (Melbourne, 1998).

Keyes, R., *The Naval Memoirs of the Admiral of the Fleet* (London, 1934).

Kinross, L., *Atatürk: Bir Milletin Yeniden Doğuşu* (İstanbul, 1981).

Kinross, L., *The Ottoman Centuries, the Rise and Fall of the Turkish Empire* (London, 1977).

Laffin, J., *Damn the Dardanelles! The Story of Gallipoli* (Sydney, 1980).

Lake, M., *A Divided Society. Tasmania during World War I* (Melbourne, 1975).

Lenin, V.I., *Sosyalizm ve Savaş* (Ankara, 1978).

Lewis, R., *Everyday Life in Ottoman Turkey* (London, 1971).

Liddle, P., *Men of Gallipoli* (London, 1976).

Lushington, R.F., *A Prisoner with the Turks 1915–1918* (London, 1923).

Mackenzie, C., *Gallipoli Memories* (London, 1929).

Malthus, C., *Anzac: A Retrospect* (Christchurch, 1965).

Mango, A., *Turkey* (London, 1968).

Marder, A.J., *From the Dardanelles to Oran* (London, 1974).

Marwick, A., *War and Social Change in the Twentieth Century* (London, 1974).

Masefield, J., *Gallipoli* (London, 1916).

McKernan, M., *The Australian People and the Great War* (Melbourne, 1980).

Moorehead, A., *Gallipoli*. Illustrated edn (Melbourne, 1975).

Muhlmann, K., *Der Kampf um die Dardanellen 1915* (Berlin, 1927).

Murray, J., *Gallipoli as I saw it* (London, 1965).

Murray, R., *Fools Rush In* (Melbourne, 1972).

Nevinson, H.W., *The Dardanelles Campaign* (London, 1918).

North, J., *Gallipoli: The Fading Vision* (London, 1936).

Önen, M., *'Birinci Dünya Harbi ve Çanakkale Boğazı'* (n.d.).

Orga, İ. and M., *Atatürk* (London, 1962).

Ortaylı, İ., *İmparatorluğun En Uzun Yüzyılı* (İstanbul, 1983).

Pedersen, P.A., *Images of Gallipoli. Photographs from the Collection of Ross J Bastiaan* (South Melbourne, 1988).

Pemberton, T.J., *Gallipoli Today* (London, 1926).

Prior, R., *Churchill's 'World Crisis' as History* (London, 1983).

Puleston, W.D., *The Dardanelles Expedition*, 2nd edn., (Annapolis, 1927).

Reid, R., *Gallipoli 1915* (Sydney, 2002).

Reid, R., *A Duty Clear Before Us* (Canberra, 2000).

Republic of Turkey, Ministry of Forestry, *The Gallipoli Peace Park International Ideas and Design Competition* (Ankara, 1997).

Robertson, J., *Anzac and Empire. The Tragedy & Glory of Gallipoli* (Port Melbourne, 1990).

Robson, L.I., *Australia and the Great War* (Melbourne, 1969).

Roland, B., *Lesbos, The Pagan Island* (Melbourne, 1963).

Sampson, A., *The Seven Sisters* (London, 1975).

Scates, B., 'In Gallipoli's Shadow: Pilgrimage, Memory, Mourning and the Great War', *Australian Historical Studies*, vol. 33, no. 119, April 2002.

Smith, T., 'Up Periscope: Submarine *AE2* Makes First Contact', *Bulletin of the Australian Institute for Maritime Archaeology*, no. 24, 2000.

Smyth, D., *Gallipoli Pilgrimage* (Melbourne, 1990).

Stegemann, B., 'We will Remember Them. The Significance of First World War Memorials in South-eastern New South Wales, 1919– 1939', *Journal of the Australian War Memorial*, No. 4, April, 1984.

TC Çalısma Bakanlığı, *Yurtdışı İşçi Sorunları '81* (Ankara, 1981).

Tugendhat, C., *Oil the Biggest Business* (London, 1968).

Tunçoku, A.M., *Anzakların Kaleminden Mehmetçik Çanakkale 1915* (Ankara, 1997).

Turkish State Institute of Statistics, *Population Census 2000* [web page] www.die.gov.tr, date accessed 11.8.2002.

Uluaslan, H., *Gallipoli Campaign* (Çanakkale, 1987).

Ünaydın, R.E., *Çanakkale'de Savaşanlar Dediler ki* (Ankara, 1960).

Union of Australian Friends of Turkey (Victorian Branch), *Newsletter,* No. 5, Special Gallipoli edition, 25 April 2001.

Upfield Secondary College, 'Trip to Turkey' (student essays) (Melbourne, 1998).

Uzuner, B., *Gelibolu ve Uzun Beyaz Bulut* (İstanbul, 2001).

von Sanders, L., *Five Years in Turkey* (Annapolis, USA, 1927).

Welborn, S., *Lords of Death: A People a Place a Legend* (Fremantle, 1982).

Wheat, J.A., 'Personal Diary' (Mitchell Library, Sydney MSS 3054 7–995C).

White, T.W., *Guests of the Unspeakable* (London, 1928).

White, M.W.D., *Australian Submarines* (Canberra, 1992).

Yerasimos, S., *Azgelişmişik Sürecinde Türkiye,* vols. 1, 2 and 3.

Young, C., et al., *Education and Employment of Turkish and Lebanese Youth* (Canberra, 1980).

# Index

recruitment of, 45–**6**
*see also* ANZAC; Anzacs; Mediterranean Expeditionary Force
Australian War Memorial, Canberra, 12
Austria–Hungary, xvii, 122

Baby 700 (Kılıç Bayır), xiii, 68, 76
Babylon, 132
Baghdad, 30, 39
Balkan Wars (1912–13), 36, 98
Bastiaan, Dr R., 14
battles (major)
    Gallipoli Campaign, xvii, 6, 7, 8, 10, 11,
        14, 15, 131, 132, 143
    land
        25 April, 62–76 *passim*
        19 May, 80–5;
        August offensive, 108–118 *passim*
        7 January 1916, 128
    naval
        3 November 1914, 52
        19 February 1915, 52
        18 March 53–5
    souvenirs from, 15, 25–7, 148, 149
    Russia, 41, 58, 130
    Suez, 41, 106, 130
Battleship Hill, 68, 76
'Beachy Bill', 120
Bean, C.E.W., 83, 108, 121, **128**
    assessment of Ottoman soldier, 121–2
Beazley, K., 150
Beijing, 16
Belike Bay, 60
Berlin, 122, 123, 124
Blackboy Hill, Western Australia, **46**
Bolshevik Revolution (1917), 130
Bomba Sırt (Quinn's Post), xiv
Bonaparte, Napoleon, 34
Bond, A., 9
Boyun (The Nek), xiv
Bracks, S., 10
British Army, 6, 7, 9, 108, 131, 132, 133
    attitude towards the enemy, 79
    fraternisation with the enemy, 119
    leadership, 103
    *see also* Mediterranean Expeditionary
        Force
Broken Hill, 47, 48
Brown. H., 89
Bulayır (Bulair), 114
Bulgaria, xvii, 36, 106, 122, 123

Byzantine Empire, xii, xvi, 30, 32

Cadry, J., **endpapers, iv**, 131, **136**
Calwell, Major General Sir C.E., 68
Campbell, A., 1, 150
Canada, 7
Çanakkale, xiii, 7, 17, 22, 33, 49, 53, 55, 73
Çanakkale, Straits of, xiii, 7, **51**
    fortifications, 33, 52
Cape Helles (Ilyasbaba Burnu), xiii, 26, 58,
    60, 69, 71, 73, 75, 76, 77, 80, 93, 94, 106,
    107, 127, 128
Carlyon, L., 19
casualties, 28
    Gallipoli campaign, total, 6
    land battles
        25 April, 74
        19 May, **82, 86**
        28 June–5 July, 103
        August offensive, 109, 118
    naval engagements, 55
cemeteries, 8, 21–2, 23, 24, 26
    pilgrimages to, 15, **16**, 23, 26, 27
Cesaret Tepe (Russell's Top), xiv
Chanak (Çanakkale), xiii
Chinese Empire, 29
Chocolate Hill (Yılgın Tepe), 118
Chunuk Bair (Conk Bayırı), xiii, 23, 25,
    **26**, 28, 65, 67, 104, 106, 111, 112, 114,
    117
Churchill, W., 40, 104
Coburg, Melbourne, 20
Colles, T., **123**
Committee of Union and Progress *see*
    Young Turks
Commonwealth War Graves Commis-
    sion, 23, 24
Conk Bayırı (Chunuk Bair), xiii, 67
Constantine, King of Greece, 124
Constantinople, xiii, xviii, 29, 30, 39, 95,
    104
    *see also* İstanbul
Council of Turkish Associations (NSW),
    11
Crimea, xviii
Crimean War, xvii, 36
Crusaders, 30
*Cumhuriyet,* 17
Curzon, Lord G.N., 132

d'Amade, General A., 60

# Index

de Robeck, Vice-Admiral J., 58
the Dardanelles (Çanakkale, Straits of),
xiii, 7, 33, 36, 43, **51**, 52, **105**, 106, 130,
133
disease, 82, 94, 99
Döver, K., 17
Döver, M., 17

Eceabat (Maidos), 23, **51**
Ecevit, B., 12
Echuca, Victoria, 147
Edirne Sırt (Mortar Ridge), xiv
Egypt, xvii, 44, 48, 56, 60
Elley, J., 137
Enver Paşa, 38, 41, 42, 43, 44, 122, 130,
131, 132
Ephesus, 30
Esad Paşa, 108, 117
evacuation, Allied, 9, **126–7**, 130, 134

Ferdinand, Archduke, 41, 45
flies, 82, 94, 101
food, 91, 94, 125
Frances, R., 21
French Army, 6, 133, 134
*see also* Mediterranean Expeditionary
Force
French Revolution, 36, 37

Gaba Tepe (Kaba Tepe), xiii, 13, 53, 60,
63, 65, 68, 120
*Gallipoli* (movie), 9, 21, 22
*Gallipoli* (book), 16
*Gallipoli Martyrs* (opera), 16–17
Gallipoli,
peninsula, 7, 9, 14, 57, 59, 61, 130, 148
Peninsula National Historical Park,
147
*see also* Çanakkale; Gelibolu
Gammage, B., 46, 113
Gelibolu (Gallipoli), xiii, 56, 58
*Gelibolu ve Uzun Beyaz Bulut*, 15
Germany, 7, 137, 138, 139
alliance with Bulgaria, 122
alliance with Ottomans, **39**, **41–2**, 130
army, 6
assessment of Ottoman Army, 57, 95
assists Ottomans, **40**, 51, 56
High Command, 104
invades Serbia, 123
navy, 43

Turkish migration to, 137–8
Gibson, M., 22
Greece, xvii
army, 133, 134
*see also* Mediterranean Expeditionary
Force
Greeks, 32, 100, 108

Hain Tepe (Plugge's Plateau), xiv, 82
Hamilton, General Sir I., 55, 57, 58, 59, 60,
75, 105, 113, 117, 149
Hawke, R.J.L., 13–14
Hell Spit (Küçük Arı Burnu), xiii
Herodotus, 38
Hikmet, N., 143
Hill 971 (Koca Çimen Tepe), xiii, 14, 104,
111, 114–16
Hittites, 30
Hobart, 1, 19
*Human Landscapes From My Country* (the
poem), 143
'Huns', 29
*see also* Germany

Ikiz Koyu (X Beach), xiv
Imbros, 62, 68
Indian Army, 6, 17
*see also* Mediterranean Expeditionary
Force
Iran, xviii
Iraq, 38, 132
Islamic Arab Empire, xvi, 30, 31
Isparta, **136**
Israel, 132
İstanbul, xiii, 22, 33, **37**, **39**, 61, 88, 89, 90,
102, 104, 106, 122, 129, 130, 133, 146
*see also* Constantinople
Italian Army, 133, 134
İzmir, 134

'Johnny Turk', 9, 119, 120
*see also* 'Abdul'; Ottoman Army
Johnston's Jolly (Kırmızı Sırt), xiii, 26, 92

Kaba Tepe (Gaba Tepe), xiii
Kanlı Sırt (Lone Pine), xiii, 9, 82, **107**,
109
Kannengeisser, Colonel H., 95, 97, 98, 101,
107, 112, 114
Kayseri, 99, 100
Kemal, Mustafa (Atatürk), 2, 7, 8, 17, **24**,

*163*

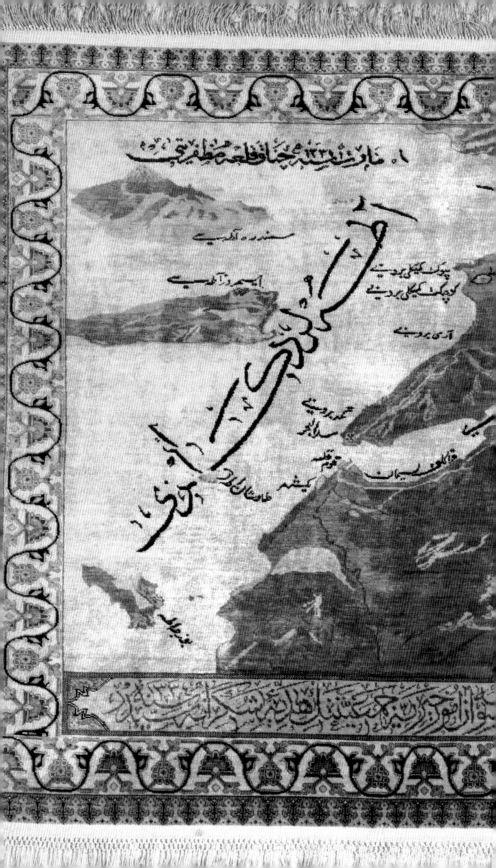